THE LONG-DISTANCE
RELATIONSHIP

SURVIVAL
GUIDE

THE **LONG-DISTANCE RELATIONSHIP**

SURVIVAL GUIDE

Secrets and Strategies from Successful Couples Who Have Gone the Distance

CHRIS BELL and **KATE BRAUER-BELL**

TEN SPEED PRESS
Berkeley | Toronto

For our son, George, and for his brother or sister on the way. Near or far, we will always love you, and we'll always hold you in our hearts.

Ten Speed Press
P.O. Box 7123
Berkeley, California 94707
www.tenspeed.com

Distributed in Australia by Simon & Schuster Australia, in Canada by Ten Speed Press Canada, in New Zealand by Southern Publishers Group, in South Africa by Real Books, and in the United Kingdom and Europe by Publishers Group UK.

Design by Catherine Jacobes Design

Library of Congress Cataloging-in-Publication Data
Bell, Chris, 1977–
The long-distance relationship survival guide / Chris Bell and Kate Brauer-Bell.
p. cm.
Includes index.
ISBN-13: 978-1-58008-714-8
ISBN-10: 1-58008-714-0
1. Dating (Social customs) 2. Long-distance relationships. I. Brauer-Bell, Kate,
1972– II. Title.
HQ801.B385 2006
646.7'7—dc22

2005026394

Printed in the United States of America
2 3 4 5 6 7 8 9 10 — 10 09 08 07 06

CONTENTS

ACKNOWLEDGMENTS

We would like to thank everyone who participated in the creation of this book, especially the many generous spirits who so openly shared their long-distance dating experiences with us. Situations presented in *The Long-Distance Relationship Survival Guide* are based on their real-life stories, although names and cities have been changed to protect individual identities, and in some cases, similar stories have been combined to illustrate a point.

In particular, we'd like to thank Paula Arriagada and Darcy Hango, Kristin and John Misso, Matt Brauer, Stan and Sarie Keller, Kelly Tucker, Ken and Kirsten Albers, Wendy and Scott McGovern, Angela Martone, and Dan and Dawn Waugh, who shared long conversations with us over the course of writing this book, opening our eyes not only to the wide range of long-distance dating situations possible, but also to the commonalities in all our experiences.

We thank Todd and Kelley Ballish for helping us through tough times in our own long-distance dating relationship. Thanks also to Katey Brichto, Jack Kerley, Susan Gfroerer, Corson Hirschfeld, John Graham, and David Borcherding for all the expert editorial advice and encouragement. Thanks to Cindy Brauer, the world's best grandma, for endless hours of babysitting while we finished our manuscript. Thanks to our agent, Debra Goldstein, and our editor, Brie Mazurek, for steering us through our first experience as authors. Most of all, thanks to Nicole Diamond Austin for believing in the need for this book and trusting that we were the people to write it.

INTRODUCTION:
Why We Wrote This Book

Not every relationship is built to last. Let's face it, with divorce rates skyrocketing and the term "commitment phobia" entering its way into mainstream English, building a successful relationship seems trickier than ever. The foundation of any good relationship depends on one thing more than any other: how well the couple in question manages to navigate the trials they face along their journey together.

No other type of dating provides as much opportunity to test the strength of a relationship's foundation as does dating long-distance. That's because the normal challenges that face any dating couple—goal setting, communication, trust, interdependence, commitment—are magnified when partners live apart for one reason or another. If your relationship is strong enough to make it through a period of long-distance, chances are it's strong enough to make it through a lot more.

We discovered the wisdom behind that statement firsthand during our own long-distance dating experience. When we started dating, we lived in cities over 450 miles apart. In fact, it was sheer coincidence that we met at all. Chris was traveling, visiting friends in Kate's hometown. That chance meeting led to a year and a half of intercity dating, followed by relocation to the same city and, ultimately, a lifetime commitment.

Of course, dating long-distance wasn't always easy. From the start, we discovered challenges same-city couples never face: When could we see each other? Who would do the traveling? Would we date exclusively? Where would each of us stay during visits? How would we get to know each other with such limited time to spend?

To be honest, neither of us set out thinking it would be great to date someone who lived so far away. But even though we figured the odds were against us, we decided to give it a go, no matter what the outcome. We knew we were in for a bumpy ride, but we didn't care. There was that indescribable *something* between us we'd not found in other relationships, and we knew we had to give the relationship a chance.

The real irony is that we had actually lived just a few blocks away from each other for more than a year and never knew it. We shopped at the same grocery, hung out at the same bookstore, and frequented the same restaurants. Our offices were within blocks of one another. To this day, we marvel that Chris had to move so far away just to meet the girl next door.

Today, when people ask the secret to our strong marriage, we always say, "Living apart for the first year and a half of our relationship." This may seem like a tongue-in-cheek response, but we couldn't be more serious about the matter. As we watch many of our friends' relationships fall victim to the everyday challenges of communication, trust, and time management, we're forever grateful we had the opportunity to get to know each other so well with so many miles between us. Happily married, we realize we might not have gotten to this point together had we not faced the challenges of a long-distance relationship. From the start, we learned to be better listeners and compassionate friends. We learned the meaning of trust and the depth of real commitment.

The nineteen months we spent dating long-distance taught us much more about relationships than we ever could have learned had we only dated in the same city. The skills we built in those months have made a lasting, positive impact on the relationship we have today. Long-distance dating was our secret to marriage success!

Unfortunately, dating across the miles wasn't as perfect as it may sound. In fact, it quickly presented a unique set of problems and challenges. We found ourselves dealing with countless misunderstandings, problems negotiating time spent together and apart, and issues revolving around effective long-distance communication. We looked for books on long-distance dating but couldn't find any that were practical or helpful in a substantial way. We wanted tactics. We wanted strategies. We wanted inside advice.

Not finding what we needed in books, we turned to other couples who had experienced long-distance relationships. All at once it seemed we were meeting more and more people who'd spent time "going the distance" before settling down. We met people who'd had unsuccessful long-distance relationships, to be sure, but we also met many whose relationships had succeeded. In fact, we met numerous married couples who, at one point or another, had to endure a period of living far apart. Everywhere we turned, we discovered couples who knew firsthand the joys and frustrations of dating across the miles.

We promised each other that if our relationship worked out for the long haul, we'd write a book to help other couples in our situation. Two years later, living in the same city and engaged to be married, we decided to do exactly that. We began to compile the knowledge we had gained in our own long-distance relationship and through our own mistakes. Realizing our experience might not apply to all couples, we started interviewing other long-distance couples, including those whose relationships had endured periods of long-distance, as well as a few individuals whose relationships didn't survive. In all, we investigated the stories behind over one hundred long-distance relationships, looking for the secrets that make them work, and the problems that most often lead to breakups. We started an online chat room for couples looking for advice on long-distance dating, and in the process we discovered an entire online community searching for the secret to successful long-distance romance.

In our research, we found that undeniable similarities surfaced again and again. These are some of the issues long-distance couples of all ages and life stages were dealing with in some form or another:

- Communicating effectively electronically and by phone

- Managing expectations and establishing mutual objectives

- Dealing with issues of trust, independence, and fidelity

- Finding enjoyment in the relationship in spite of the distance involved

- Using effective time-management strategies to help balance the demands of travel and home

- Avoiding the fantasy and getting down to what's real

- Creating intimacy in spite of physical distance and infrequent visits

- Successfully making the transition from long-distance to same-city dating

Through interviews, conversations, and our own experiences, we've come up with practical strategies and honest advice for anyone involved in, or even considering, a long-distance relationship.

If you're one of those people, you're not alone. In fact, in 2003, researchers at Purdue University reported an estimated seven hundred thousand to one million long-distance marriages in the United States and another one million to one and a half million unmarried couples dating long-distance. To find examples, you need not look farther than your local college campus, where, the same study indicates, one in four college students is involved in a long-distance relationship. The overwhelming number of websites, chat rooms, and web rings devoted to long-distance dating is testimony to the rising popularity of the long-distance relationship phenomenon. Just enter the words *long-distance relationship* into any search engine, and you'll quickly discover that hundreds of thousands of people are having long-distance relationships. They're not only having them; they're talking about them. And they're looking for advice.

The Long-Distance Relationship Survival Guide is the book we wished we had when we were starting out—a practical guide to navigating the often-bumpy waters of long-distance dating. While it's true that not every dating couple is looking for a lifelong commitment, this book is written for those who hope to build a serious relationship. Chances are, that's why you bought this book. Without a doubt, long-distance relationships can be some of the most difficult to make work. They can also be some of the most rewarding.

Each chapter of *The Long-Distance Relationship Survival Guide* presents real-life situations experienced by the couples we interviewed. For some, the distance in their relationship began after relocation, college admission, or military deployment. For others, the relationship began as a long-distance situation, the couple having met online or while traveling for business. The people we spoke with came from all walks of life and had varying levels of life experience. From college students discovering the ins and outs of their first significant relationship to professionals at the top of their field taking a second (or third or fourth) chance on love, they all had different stories, but the lessons were often much the same. Although names and some details have been changed, the experiences described are real, as are each couple's results.

In the first chapter, we'll examine the different situations that lead to long-distance relationships, including cyberdating, military service, business travel, relocation, and school. We'll also discuss the differences between living far apart on a temporary versus a long-term basis, as well as the importance of ensuring that both parties have similar expectations regarding the distance as it pertains to their relationship. We'll begin to look at some of the fundamental differences in issues faced by couples whose relationships start out long-distance as opposed to those whose relationships become long-distance after some time in the same locale. Finally, touching on the basic challenges that all long-distance relationships present, we'll talk about the intense emotional bond possible with a successful long-distance relationship, and we'll explore why many couples find it worth all the trouble and how they make it work.

In chapter 2, we'll discuss one of the key principles of successful long-distance dating—effective communication. Of course, the ability to communicate is important in any relationship, but a long-distance couple must develop excellent oral and written communication skills if their relationship is to thrive. In this chapter, we'll suggest some solid communication strategies couples can apply every day, and we'll provide examples of effective long-distance communication by email and phone.

Goal setting is a valuable skill in any relationship, and its value for long-distance couples shouldn't be overlooked. In chapter 3, we'll discuss the importance of setting mutual goals and provide examples of the kinds of goals you might want to consider for your long-distance relationship. We'll also supply plenty of practical techniques for goal setting, and share sound advice for working as a team, even across the miles.

Trust is the cornerstone of any successful long-distance dating relationship; without it, partners won't feel comfortably secure in their relationship while they're apart. That's why chapter 4 is dedicated to this important subject, with special attention to issues of fidelity and honesty. We'll examine the meaning of trust, and we'll give you some warning signs for determining when it may be best not to give your trust, and when the wisest thing to do just may be to walk away.

Long-distance dating is difficult—sometimes nearly impossible. But with a little creativity and a childlike sense of play, even the impossible suddenly becomes easier to bear. Chapter 5 focuses on a very important (and all too often overlooked) element of long-distance relationship—creativity. In this chapter, we'll show you how real couples used creativity to enhance their long-distance dating experience, and we'll give you lots of fun ideas to get your creative juices flowing.

Unlike same-city relationships, long-distance dating comes with its own unique logistical considerations. Chapter 6 addresses time management, relationship negotiation, and other practical aspects of maintaining a balanced, happy dating life long-distance.

Because it can be difficult to maintain a sense of authenticity in a long-distance relationship, chapter 7 offers advice for making the most of your limited time together. Here we'll explore what it means to keep a relationship real and provide strategies you can apply to your own relationship.

Chapter 8 discusses the issues of sex and intimacy in long-distance relationships and explores how the distance can both enhance and hinder a caring dating experience. Since every relationship approaches intimacy differently, we'll explore these issues as they relate to couples with varying levels of sexual involvement.

Though you may think the challenges of long-distance dating end when a couple makes the move to the same city, this isn't always the case. Often this is precisely when the greatest challenges present themselves. In chapter 9, we'll talk about the eventual decision to relocate for the sake of being together, including potential pitfalls and strategies for making the transition as smooth as possible.

The truth is, these days it's not uncommon to meet couples whose relationship, at one time or another, could have been classified as long-distance. With so many of us traveling for business or school and meeting people in a variety of places far from home, the likelihood of developing a long-distance romance increases each day. The Internet has been another contributing factor in changing the way we date. Now more than ever, couples are meeting online in chat rooms or on singles sites and getting to know each other through email and instant chat. Beyond that, the ongoing service of military men and women overseas has become a huge contributor to the long-distance dating phenomenon. In fact, more and more of today's relationships involve some amount of long-distance courtship. This book isn't exclusively devoted to any particular type of intercity dating relationship. In fact, if you've ever even considered long-distance love, this book is for you.

These relationships are not easy, but take heart—they can work. Our marriage and countless successful relationships like it are living proof. We learned a lot in the eighteen months we lived apart, and we hope that by sharing our experience—and the experiences of many other successful couples—we can help you discover the joy and happiness your own successful long-distance relationship may have in store!

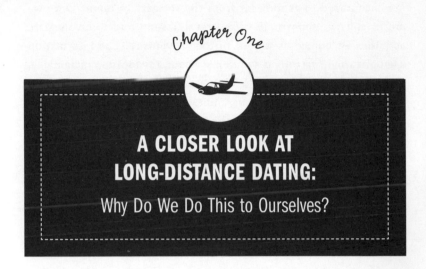

Chapter One

A CLOSER LOOK AT LONG-DISTANCE DATING:
Why Do We Do This to Ourselves?

Once upon a time, the vast majority of us spent our entire lives, or at least a significant portion of our lives, in one hometown. Cultural differences, limited resources, and the expense of travel meant that most of us seldom met others from outside our own area. When we did meet someone from a distant city, communication and travel barriers generally discouraged the formation of a significant relationship.

Happily, that's no longer the case. If we are college bound, we are encouraged to venture far from the security of home. Once we are in college, opportunities for travel abroad and intercollegiate activities encourage us toward further adventure. The information age opens a virtual job market in just about any location imaginable, and when we first enter the workforce, opportunities for travel generally increase. For many of us, military service requires long periods of time away from home and family. For others, company mergers and business development in a global economy lead to transfers and long commutes. Many of us—single or attached—hop on a plane weekly as part of a regular routine. In many cases, even our retirements are spent exploring new terrain.

Our academic and business lives aren't the only aspects we've seen become global in recent years. The increase in Internet usage in the 1990s led to a new phenomenon in dating that's even more popular today—cyberdating. People of all ages and backgrounds are going online to find partners—meeting in chat rooms or through personal ads—and often choosing to meet face-to-face.

The Internet, along with fiercely competitive long-distance rates and increasingly common cell phone use, has made seemingly impossible relationships much more manageable. Formerly unimaginable long-distance connections are not only possible—in some cases, they're preferable to same-city dating relationships. How can this be? Well, from the start of their relationship, long-distance couples have many opportunities to learn and grow together, opportunities that some same-city couples who have dated for years never have.

The very fact that you picked up this book means you're one of the millions of people involved in or, at the very least, considering a long-distance relationship. Hopefully, this book will help you learn more about the potential challenges, pitfalls, and rewards of long-distance dating so you can decide if this kind of relationship is for you and, if so, what steps you can take to help ensure smooth sailing on the voyage ahead. With a little luck and a lot of hard work, you just may find that your destination is long-term relationship success.

FINDING SUCCESS IN LONG-DISTANCE LOVE

When Linda and George met, George had recently relocated from Amarillo to Denver to work for a large manufacturing corporation. Linda was in Amarillo building a strong reputation as a local journalist. Both had thriving careers that kept them tied to the towns they were in, and each had become accustomed to an independent lifestyle.

The two met at a party one weekend when George had returned to Amarillo to visit some friends. "I didn't even admit to Linda that I lived in another city until after nearly two full weeks of emailing and online chats," he says. "I was afraid she wouldn't be interested if she knew how far away I lived." He may have been right. The idea of long-distance dating isn't always appealing. The infrequency of visits and the difficulty inherent in communication can make a couple's chances of success seem daunting at best. George explains he considered his choice not to come clean with Linda right away a necessary preemptive move. "I wanted to give her the chance to get to know me before she decided whether or not it was worth giving the relationship a shot."

Apparently, it worked. "By the time he told me where he lived, both of us were already too hooked on each other to let the distance stop us," Linda recalls. And so began their journey into the world of long-distance dating.

For a year and a half, they traveled back and forth every other weekend, enduring airport delays or the eight-hour drive just for the chance to see each other for a day or two. "We learned to put up with long periods of not seeing each other, endless misunderstandings over email or phone, skyrocketing long-distance bills, and lonely Saturday nights wishing we could be together," Linda says. But for all the negatives, there were positive aspects as well. "We also learned to communicate our feelings clearly, support each other through hard times, and really make the most of our time together."

George and Linda discovered that little-known fact that many couples involved in long-distance relationships learn—in some strange way, distance can actually be good for a relationship. In fact, the struggles a long-distance couple must face together can help strengthen the fiber of their relationship, better preparing both partners for future challenges, whether those challenges are faced together or as

Ten Signs You May Not Be Cut Out for a Long-Distance Romance

Not sure if this sort of relationship is for you? The following signs just might indicate you're better cut out for "local love":

1. You can't stand talking on the phone.

2. You've always meant to get on the Internet, but you can't find your computer's On switch.

3. The idea of traveling more than once or twice a year gives you motion sickness.

4. You feel incomplete without a boyfriend or girlfriend around at all times.

5. Physical intimacy is so important to you that if you can't have it on a regular basis, you'll be tempted to look outside the relationship.

6. You're drawn to the idea of long-distance dating because it will finally let you live that double life you've been dreaming of. (Believe it or not, there are a lot of people out there who use long-distance relationships to cheat on their partner or spouse. It almost always blows up in their faces in the end.)

7. You rely on body language to get your point across in discussions or arguments and would be lost without it.

8. You think relationships should be all fun and no work. (Trust us, long-distance dating can be fun, but it also takes a huge effort.)

9. You're only mildly interested in the person you're considering dating long-distance.

10. You believe chivalry is dead and that true romance exists only in fairy tales.

individuals. The distance in George and Linda's relationship meant more time spent apart, a factor they now say taught them to place a higher value on their time together. It also helped each partner more fully appreciate the other. Of course, George and Linda didn't enter into their relationship knowing this from the get-go. In fact, each now admits that, while they were dating, it wasn't always easy to see the positive side of long-distance courtship.

Intercity dating is difficult; that much is certain. So why are so many of us willing to give it a shot? Typically, willingness to involve ourselves in something this challenging indicates that we see the potential for something wonderful to develop. It's a lot easier to find ourselves dating someone we're not really into if that person lives right down the street than it is to devote hours of driving or flying time and huge phone bills to someone who only mildly piques our interest.

In our case, neither one of us would have ever considered even casual long-distance dating, let alone having a serious long-distance relationship, were it not for what can only be described as love at first sight. If that sounds ridiculously romantic, perhaps it is. But this sort of belief in romance is an absolute prerequisite for long-distance dating success. For us, our romance was the fire that fueled our often-difficult journey toward long-term commitment. From the moment we met, we began an adventure that would become the greatest learning experience of our lives. Intercity dating was never anything either of us would have described as ideal, but there was something special between us that was too hard to ignore.

We met purely by chance, although we had at one time lived in the same city. A few weeks before we met, Chris left Cincinnati to accept a job in Greenville, South Carolina. The job was great, but he missed the friends he'd left behind. On a weekend visit to Ohio to see "the guys," serendipity played its hand, and somehow we ended

Communication Starters

Here are some questions to help facilitate communication
with your partner about your long-distance relationship. Give
thought not only to your responses, but to your partner's
responses as well. You may be surprised at what you
discover:

- Why did you choose to date long-distance?

- What is the best part of your relationship?

- What is the most difficult aspect of your relationship?

- Is having a long-distance relationship more or less
  difficult than you thought it would be when you first
  started dating? Why?

- What is the most significant potential pitfall you believe
  you might encounter in long-distance dating?

- What makes your long-distance relationship worth it?

up in the same dance club, both equally uncomfortable with the
smoky, "meat market" atmosphere. We struck up a conversation, and
there was a spark. It was one of those moments of true clarity, when
life's calling seems abundantly clear.

Our first date was two weeks later. Chris drove up on a Saturday
and stayed in a bachelor friend's spare room. The two of us went to
see a movie and then grabbed a bite to eat at a nearby bar and grill.
The place wasn't too crowded—just right for conversation. We talked
for hours, discussing everything from our family lives, to politics and
religion, to our dreams for the future, and only left when the servers

began putting chairs up on the tables. It was clear to both of us that we shared something special. We decided that in the beginning Chris would do the traveling. We dated exclusively from the start, but he stayed with friends on his visits. We relied on lots of phone calls and emails to get to know each other during our courtship. And through it all, we found ourselves falling more and more deeply in love.

So for us, the decision to date long-distance wasn't really much of a decision at all—it was something we fell into and decided to make the best of. We knew we wanted to be together and that the distance between us was just an obstacle we'd have to overcome. Not all long-distance couples set out with such conviction, but it certainly does help.

For anyone considering long-distance dating, this is a factor worth some consideration. If either or both of you have only luke-warm feelings toward the other or toward the relationship, then the extra effort intercity dating requires may not be worth your while. If, on the other hand, you're each passionate about the other and about the relationship, then no amount of distance will likely keep you apart. And isn't that the sort of relationship we all deserve?

WHEN ONE PARTNER MOVES AWAY

Sometimes a couple might transition from same-city to long-distance dating due to a career change, school, or some other factor. Mitch met his wife, Erin, when they both lived in the same small town in Virginia. The two dated for some time, and then Erin began medical school in a city 250 miles away. Although he cared for Erin deeply, Mitch didn't want to move. He says he just wasn't ready to leave. Mitch was happy in Virginia in the same town as all of his friends and family, and where he had a very good job. At the same time, he knew he wasn't ready to simply give up on the relationship. He had dated long-distance before and decided this would be a reasonable way to continue seeing Erin. The two kept dating, seeing each other at least three times each month.

Soon, something became remarkably clear in their relationship, something they'd been uncertain of before. Not long after Erin relocated, Mitch recognized how much he missed her. Suddenly, he knew without a doubt that he wanted to be with her long term. As their commitment to the relationship—and to each other—continued to deepen, Erin and Mitch came to fully realize just how strongly they wanted to be together. This realization helped them through difficult times. "I knew that the long-distance aspect of our relationship wouldn't last forever, and that something had to give," Mitch says now.

It's been said that "absence makes the heart grow fonder." This may be true. Perhaps more likely, however, is that distance provides the psychological space needed for an honest evaluation of a relationship. For Erin and Mitch, this certainly proved to be the case. Mitch proposed just six months after Erin moved, and the couple married six months after that. He was able to find a job near her medical school, and when she graduated the newlyweds moved back to Virginia, near the family and friends they both cared about so much.

Talia and Jack also faced the transition to a long-distance dating relationship. They started seeing each other while attending law school in Louisiana. After graduation, the couple found themselves facing financial difficulties. There were school loans to be paid, and although they had both done well in law school, they'd had difficulty finding jobs. Talia finally found a good position in Washington, D.C., while Jack's career track led him to a corporate position in Houston. The couple decided to continue seeing each other long-distance. At that point, they realized they were not yet ready to get married, and neither one felt they could afford to turn down such terrific job opportunities.

Talia's position required a two-year commitment, so she and Jack agreed to date long-distance for two years with the end goal of eventually being together. This was Talia's second long-distance relationship. Before meeting Jack, she had dated a man who lived in Europe but ended the relationship because she felt she had little reason to invest the effort it required. With Jack, things were different. Both knew the relationship was worth the investment.

> *Tip:* **A strong relationship will be strong enough to survive just about any challenge—even distance. So if you discover your relationship can't survive a period of living far apart, don't feel too bad. As much as it may hurt to admit it, it's probably better to move on.**

Nevertheless, the change wasn't easy. The couple discovered how lonely a long-distance relationship could be. They missed waking up together, doing the grocery shopping together, and the day-to-day details of same-city dating. "He had become such an integral part of my life," Talia says, "and I really missed sharing those things."

But in spite of the difficulties, Jack says their relationship worked because they never lost sight of their plans to one day be together. "The end objective has always remained the same, but how we went about getting there has changed over the course of the relationship." Today, Jack and Talia are newlyweds, still living in separate cities while Talia begins her job hunt in Houston. While the couple admits the commute is a challenge, they've found ways to make it work, at least until a job opportunity for Talia presents itself.

SEEING THINGS MORE CLEARLY . . . AT A DISTANCE

Not everyone is eager to try dating long-distance when one partner's career or educational goals lead that person to a new city. For many couples, such a transition can signal the end of an otherwise good relationship. Conversely, some couples intend to stop dating when one or both partners move away but find themselves inextricably drawn back into the relationship in spite of the distance.

In the case of Dave and Shelly, when Shelly took a job out of the country, Dave decided to end their dating relationship. It was a difficult decision, and the two remained friends. In just four months' time, Shelly came to the conclusion that she didn't want to live without him, and she made a commitment to him to return within a year. That commitment was enough to convince Dave that the relationship was worth continuing. The two began dating again, long-distance, and building their relationship. This time, the relationship was moving toward a common goal—the goal of being together. Eventually Shelly found a job in the states just two hours' drive from Dave's hometown. Two years later, they married. "Being away from each other for that long helped us better see our feelings for each other," she says. "The distance allowed us to each appreciate what we were missing."

Often the strength of a relationship is put to the test when one partner is offered a job in another city, when education goals lead someone far from home, when military service requires foreign duty, or when one partner's career requires a great deal of travel. Such was the case for Sharon and Jim. When Jim accepted a position as a business consultant, he suddenly found himself required to work long hours and travel to cities all over the globe. Sharon felt frustrated to be alone so much, but she supported his decision to take the position, recognizing that it would be an important stepping-stone for his career. The couple agreed that Jim would work the consulting job for two years but afterward would settle into a position that allowed him to spend more time at home. The compromise was difficult for both, but on the positive side, they were able to view it as an expression of their growing commitment to one another.

Jim says Sharon's support of his career marked an important change in their relationship. "She was willing to put her faith in me, and in turn, I was willing to commit to settling down after two years." Today, the couple is engaged to be married, and Jim is searching for a position that puts him closer to home.

For military couples, deployment can require long periods of separation. In a dating relationship, one partner's deployment can lead to feelings of anxiety, guilt, fear, and frustration for both, particularly if the other partner is a civilian who has never been exposed

Develop a Relationship . . . with Yourself

If you or your partner suddenly moves away, you will undoubtedly find yourself with more time on your hands. Empty hours can lead to loneliness and despair, so this is not the time to sit around and wait for something good to happen. Look at it this way: the weeks or months you have to spend away from your partner will pass more quickly if you fill them with positive activities.

This is the time to discover a new hobby or rediscover an old one. Take up journaling, painting, or writing poetry. Learn all that you can about who you are as an individual, and you'll have more to offer your relationship.

to a military lifestyle. Regardless, a commitment to duty demands enduring such separation, and this sense of duty often extends to the civilian partner as well. Karen, a civilian employee at an air force base in Ohio, has been involved in a dating relationship with an air force pilot for six months. She says she knew from the beginning of their relationship that her boyfriend, Tony, might someday be called to duty. When the time came for him to ship out, her commitment only deepened. "He risks his life every day for me and for everyone else in our country," says Karen. "I want him to know there will be someone back home waiting for him when he returns."

Erica and Jeff, who have been married for seven years at the time of this writing, had been dating on and off for two years when Jeff left Cleveland, their hometown, and accepted a job near Santa Fe. When Jeff moved, Erica figured the relationship was over. But the two kept in contact and ultimately continued dating. Jeff moved back a year later, and they were married a year after that.

For Jeff and Erica, dating long-distance helped build a commitment that had been lacking when they dated in the same city. In fact, they had experienced difficulties around commitment long before Jeff moved to New Mexico, breaking up and getting back together several times. "Sometimes it takes a big move to show you what you have," he says now.

Erica believes the distance in their relationship was a deciding factor in helping them take their relationship to the next level. "The distance actually kept us together because we talked so much. It also made Jeff realize he didn't want to live without me for the rest of his life."

Like Jeff and Erica, many couples discover that long-distance dating can be a good way to help clarify their feelings for one another. This was true for Carlos and Rhonda, who shared a similar experience when Rhonda, a human resources executive for an international firm, accepted a position that took her out of her hometown in New Jersey to Ontario, Canada. Carlos didn't think he could continue dating her when she was that far away. "To be honest with you, I think I felt insulted that she just got up and left," he admits now. "I felt like there was a lot of pressure to propose to her if I didn't want her to leave, and I wasn't ready to do that. So I just said to myself, 'Okay, well, this relationship wasn't meant to be.' But as soon as she was gone, I realized how much I missed her."

In the beginning, Carlos dealt with his loneliness by dating other people. "There was one girl I dated for a couple of months. I kind of liked her, but there was just something missing. She talked to me about it one night, and I realized I just didn't care about her the way I cared about Rhonda." The experience led him to do a little soul-searching, and that's when he realized he wanted to pursue a relationship with his former girlfriend even though she was now considerably farther away.

When Carlos called Rhonda, she was surprised but happy. "I never wanted to break up with him in the first place, but I figured if he really loved me, he would make a commitment to me and the relationship."

Eventually that's exactly what he did. The two dated long-distance for another three months, and then Carlos began looking for a job in Canada. No sooner had he started to look than Rhonda realized she really wanted to be back home. She was approved for a transfer to New Jersey, and the two were engaged shortly after.

Of course, breakup stories don't always have happy endings. Take the example of Derek and Katie. Derek accepted a two-year teaching position in Norway while his college sweetheart, Katie, kept the home fires burning in Illinois. During the course of his work overseas, Derek returned home once every few months, generally for a week at a time. On his trips home, he found himself wanting to spend more time with family and friends than with Katie. He says that instead of absence making his heart grow fonder, with time he found himself growing more distant from the relationship. "Finally, it got to the point where I realized I'd rather spend my holiday traveling around Europe than come home for the summer. That's when I knew the relationship wasn't going anywhere."

The decision to stop seeing Katie was, in Derek's words, "difficult but necessary." The distance separating him from his longtime girlfriend gave him the space he needed to see that it was time to move on. So, although they may not have had the happy ending most couples dream about, they were fortunate in that the distance helped clarify that the relationship wasn't meant to last. This made the decision to break it off far easier than it might have been if the two were still entwined in each other's day-to-day lives.

Lou and Mindy had a similar experience when Lou, an airline pilot, lost his job due to industry cutbacks. To make ends meet, he left his hometown in Connecticut and moved to Florida to accept a teaching position at a flight school. Mindy, his girlfriend of over five years, stayed behind. The couple's plan was for Lou to return once the job market improved. But the distance between them helped him clarify his feelings about the relationship; ultimately, he ended up breaking things off.

Mindy says she felt devastated at first, but that over time she was actually grateful for the experience. "Things weren't that great between us, but we had always just settled for it and tried to make the best of it," she says. "When Lou broke up with me, I felt like it was the end of the world—we had been together for so long. But after several months, I started to see that the breakup was really for the best. I'm glad his move helped bring us to that point sooner rather than later, because we would have broken up eventually, even if we had still been living in the same place." Today, Mindy is involved in a good relationship. She says that she and her new partner want more of the same things in life. "It took a radical change to shake things up and help Lou and me see that we'd really be better off apart."

Stories like this are more common than you might think. We spoke to many people who had folded to the pressures of long-distance dating, throwing in the towel on a relationship they might have continued more easily had both people been in the same city. So if dating long-distance can cause so many couples to break up, is it really worth it? We think so.

Consider this: Most of us know at least one older couple who have been happily married for decades. Chances are, if you were to ask them their secret to a successful marriage, they would tell you they simply couldn't imagine their lives without one another. Isn't that the kind of love we all search for? The clarity that comes with long-distance dating helps us identify whether or not we've found that kind of special relationship.

With so many miles keeping you and your partner apart, at some point you'll inevitably find yourself wondering if you'd be better off alone. If you're very lucky and you *have* found a deep, genuine love, both you and your partner will come to the conclusion that life is better when you're together, and the two of you will easily resolve to commit to the relationship. If, on the other hand, you and your partner are not both equally deeply in love, one or both of you will likely come to the conclusion that life would be better without the difficulties of a long-distance commitment. And while that sort of realization is undoubtedly a painful one, we believe a discovery of that nature is actually quite fortunate, because the sooner you recognize that a relationship isn't right for you, the sooner you'll be able to move on with life and find the relationship that is.

After all this talk of breakups, you'll be pleased to know there is a silver lining to the dark cloud of discontent that has the potential to hang ominously over long-distance couples. With your relationship, and your commitment, put to the test in a long-distance dating situation, you won't have to wonder for long whether or not it has real potential for success. We believe couples who date long-distance for a period of time before settling down together probably have a greater chance at making their same-city relationship work, because they've already dealt with so many of the major issues that threaten to break couples up: loneliness, jealousy, communication difficulties, financial strain, and outside obligations. In many ways, long-distance dating helps open the door to a truly solid, committed relationship. As one woman told us, "If your relationship is strong enough to survive long-distance, then it can survive just about anything." And if it isn't strong enough, wouldn't you rather find out now, no matter how hard that might be?

Commitment is vital to the success of any relationship, but this is especially true for relationships that span many miles, since maintaining such a relationship naturally requires a great deal more work, planning, and effort. If your commitment is strong enough for a long-distance relationship, just think of all of the challenges you'll be able to overcome together in the years ahead.

DISCOVERING INDEPENDENCE THROUGH A LONG-DISTANCE CONNECTION

The very structure of a long-distance relationship appeals to some people because of the freedom it allows. For those of us who are uncertain about our own independence outside of a relationship, geographical space can provide psychological space as well—an unexpected benefit during the course of a long-distance relationship.

This was certainly the case in our long-distance relationship. We had both had our share of failed same-city relationships before meeting each other, and Chris had even broken off a prior relationship when the woman he was seeing moved away. But neither of us had ever experienced a serious, loving relationship with so much room for independence and individual growth. Although it could be lonely at times, our long-distance courtship also taught us an incredible lesson: that we could be completely in love and completely self-reliant at the same time. It's a discovery we've carried into our relationship today, strengthening us not only as individuals, but also as a couple.

Stacy and Greg started dating after meeting in an online chat room for pet lovers. Attracted to Stacy's funny, caring spirit, Greg wanted to meet her in person. When he found out she lived in Pensacola, he decided he'd visit her during a conference he was scheduled to attend that spring. The two met and hit it off from the start. Although Greg lived in West Texas, they decided to start a long-distance relationship. After dating each other in cities over eight hundred miles apart for nearly two years, they eventually tied the knot. Happily married, today they live together Florida.

Although she admits the long-distance relationship was difficult, Stacy says she wouldn't have changed it for the world. She says the distance gave her a chance to discover more about herself than she would have otherwise. She admits that in previous dating relationships she would rely on the man in her life to take care of tasks such as car maintenance or simple home repairs. With Greg visiting only once every few weeks, Stacy didn't want to waste their precious time together asking him for help with projects she knew she could figure out how to do on her own. "I learned to rely on myself better for the things I needed, rather than go running to my boyfriend every time I had a problem I thought I couldn't solve. I learned to be more resourceful." She says a real turning point in her life came when her dishwasher wasn't working properly and needed a simple repair. She researched the repair on the Internet, purchased the part she needed, and made the fix herself. "I never knew I was capable of doing something like that on my own. It's a great feeling."

Greg, who had been involved in a steady stream of serious relationships since his college days, says the two years they spent apart gave him a chance to feel like he'd better experienced his single years. "There's something to be said for having the opportunity to spend time on your own. Although the years we were apart were difficult and presented a lot of unusual challenges, they also allowed us each a chance to experience some aspects of what life is like as a single person." He admits that he didn't see this as a benefit during the time they were dating. In fact, he says the distance never seemed like anything but heartache at the time. It was only after the fact that he realized he'd actually enjoyed, at least in part, his time as an "independent man."

Greg is quick to point out that independence never led to infidelity. Instead, he says it deepened his commitment to Stacy because he missed her so much. Evenings were often lonely, and Greg's thoughts turned toward making a lasting commitment. The things he learned about himself during their years apart helped shape him into a better man when it came time to commit and settle down. He credits his time apart from Stacy with helping him evolve into a more well-rounded person. When they were finally able to be together, both Greg and Stacy had more to offer the relationship than they might have if they had never had the experience of dating long-distance.

Greg is glad he had that opportunity, even though he was lonely at times. "That kind of solitude gave me a chance to develop my own interests. I read a lot during those two years, a lot more than I have time for now, and I even learned to cook. I don't think I'd have done that if I'd had a girlfriend in the same town."

Communication Starters

How does distance affect your relationship? Use the questions below to start a dialogue with your partner:

- Would you be interested in your current relationship if your partner lived in your city?

- What would be different about your relationship if you and your partner lived in the same city? What would be the same?

- What would make the circumstances of your long-distance relationship easier? What would make them harder?

If you're involved in a long-distance relationship, you can learn to view this time in your life as an opportunity to cultivate self-awareness and develop a sense of self-reliance. This is a real chance to focus on personal growth. Use the free time you have during days and weeks apart to concentrate on areas of your life you would like to enhance, change, or improve. While this advice may seem best suited to young couples just starting out in college or careers, it's equally valid for older couples further along on their life's journey. No matter what your age, growing as an individual will make you stronger; and as a stronger person, you'll have more to contribute to your relationship, and all your relationships throughout your life.

Greg and Stacy never intended to use the distance to help them grow as individuals, but that was the effect. In other cases, couples think about, and even discuss, this benefit before deciding to date across the miles.

As we alluded to above, for some young couples a temporary separation, such as the separation following college graduation, for instance, can provide a vital opportunity for personal growth. Jenna, a twenty-five-year-old graphic designer, says she wasn't yet ready to commit to marrying her boyfriend, Kyle, when they graduated, but she also wasn't willing to give up the relationship. Perhaps not surprisingly, we found this situation to be common for couples at the start of life after college. Jenna explained her feelings to Kyle, and they decided dating long-distance would be the best solution. The couple lived in separate cities for a year and a half before they found employment in the same town. Much to her surprise, Jenna, who was twenty-two at the time, found that the months apart were actually freeing in many ways. Entering the professional and social world on her own, she was able to discover what she wanted from life without the normal distractions of same-city dating.

Kyle made discoveries of his own during the time apart from his girlfriend. The independence he felt in the long-distance relationship challenged him to carry on the daily activities of life without procrastination. "I was able to do things I wanted to do without having to wait for Jenna," he says. "At the same time, I discovered that I depended on her a lot when she was around; without her there every day, I quickly learned that I needed to depend on myself."

But as we said, self-reliance is not just for the very young. Sometimes, particularly after a painful divorce or breakup, independence is an appealing motivator in choosing to date long-distance. Dating someone in another city can provide the breathing room many people feel they need after the loss of a partner. Intercity dating can, in many ways, offer the best of both worlds—someone to love, confide in, and enjoy, along with the space and time to heal from a previous loss and to learn to stand on your own two feet again. A long-distance relationship can provide some people with the sense of autonomy they need in order to learn about themselves, or to function as independent individuals.

Vic, a realtor in Wisconsin, and Betsy, a social worker in Illinois, discovered for themselves how rewarding a long-distance relationship could be. The two met through an online dating service. When they first began seeing each other, they intended to keep the relationship casual. Neither wanted to be tied down in an intercity relationship because, at the time, neither believed it would be possible to develop a meaningful connection with someone who lived so far away. Although both had doubts about the relationship's potential, each recognized something special in the other. They decided to get to know each other and see how things worked out.

Tip: **Email provides a great vehicle for getting to know someone new. It's often easier to open up and share parts of ourselves through the reflective process of writing than in an impromptu conversation.**

The two began talking on the phone and through email more and more frequently, sharing their deepest thoughts and feelings. "It was, in some ways, easier to talk to Vic because he was so far away," Betsy says. "I know it sounds like a contradiction, but it's true. We wrote each other long emails every day. We fell in love with each other through the words we were writing." Eventually Vic and Betsy made the commitment to live in the same city. Today, they say taking a chance on love was the best decision they ever made.

GOING THE DISTANCE AND REAPING THE REWARDS

Of course, dating long-distance isn't easy. But there's something else about long-distance relationships you need to know: they can be fun.

That's right. Loving someone far away gives you plenty of room to be creative, and it can allow for great travel opportunities and shared adventures. For many of us, long-distance dating brings unexpected benefits. Lots of couples admit that, although their time apart was challenging, they would not change their experience for the world. In the words of one woman we spoke with, now happily married, "Living away from each other taught us to value one another and to fully recognize how lucky we are to be together."

Long-distance relationships are a challenge. They call us to rise above ourselves, to reach for heights we might not otherwise reach. So why do we do this to ourselves? We do it because we see the potential for love, maybe even long-term commitment. And, successful or otherwise, these relationships give us a window into ourselves. We learn the depth of our strength, the breadth of our self-reliance, and, most of all, the distances we will travel for the promise of love.

Chapter Two

COMMUNICATION:
Paving the Road to Success

Justin and Liz dated during their first two years of college. In their third year, the couple moved into a small apartment together. Living together was a comfortable adjustment, and they quickly found it suited their relationship well. Liz took on many of the daily household chores, while Justin quickly adapted to preparing meals and doing laundry. The two made a great team. After graduation, when Justin left for a job in France, the couple felt they had lost not only the comfort of physical closeness, but an entire way of life. With things so different in their relationship, Liz returned to her home state of Washington to search for a job, and Justin realized things would never be quite the same.

For Justin, the thought of moving overseas and leaving behind someone he'd grown so close to over four years was nerve-racking. Liz, on the other hand, initially thought the transition wouldn't be too difficult. The couple had discussed their options and had agreed the separation wouldn't last more than a year, which they figured would be just long enough for Justin to experience life overseas and return to the states with an interesting credit to his résumé. Soon, however, trouble set in.

Justin and Liz had been used to daily communication, but now, due to constraints of finances and the difference of nine time zones, daily phone calls were impossible. Justin found himself worried about the relationship and missing the regular contact he used to share with his girlfriend. The sense of loss was devastating. He was overcome by a feeling of loneliness and a fear that the new job Liz had found would mean she'd have no time left for him. Although the couple's relationship managed to survive the yearlong separation, at times the challenges of remote communication were extremely difficult for both partners. Now living in the same town and engaged to be married, the two say the time they spent dating each other long-distance taught them things about strong communication that continue to serve their relationship today.

Inarguably, the ability to communicate effectively is one of the key determining factors for success in any romantic relationship. The comfort and freedom to express our feelings to a caring partner is one of the major reasons people seek connections in life. Good communication skills take on an even greater importance in long-distance dating. It's easy to see why, since lack of daily contact can make it difficult to discern the meaning behind something written in an email or spoken carelessly during a late-night call. After all, local couples are blessed with the familiarity of regular contact and the ability to understand each other more fully through the experience of body language.

When you can't see the other person's facial expressions, body posture, or general mood, it's all too easy to misunderstand a casual comment as hurtful, or a lack of verbal response as a lack of caring. Let's face it: it's far easier to read someone's intentions when you can see the expression in his or her eyes than it is to correctly discern the true emotion behind a few words quickly typed in an email during the workday, or to accurately gauge tone of voice during a late-night call. What may seem like a rude remark in an email or instant message may just be a sign that the sender is particularly busy or caught off guard. Likewise, that snappish tone you detected on the phone may only be the sound of someone who's tired and ready for bed. More often than not, these kinds of concerns simply signal that both partners need to develop more effective methods of oral and written communication.

We've all experienced miscommunications over email or the telephone. When these methods become a couple's primary vehicles for connecting with one another, such miscommunications are even more dangerous. But as much as these glitches in communication may seem like insurmountable hurdles, conquering them can lead to an even richer understanding of one another, an understanding that can help the relationship flourish in the long run.

If you're considering whether or not long-distance dating is for you, one thing you must ask yourself is this: how much time will you and your partner have, realistically, to devote to communication? Oftentimes the answer to this one question will be a key determinant of a long-distance couple's success. Beyond the matter of time availability, you should also consider whether or not you and your partner are equally willing to invest that time toward communication. Remember, even if you and your partner each have plenty of time on your hands, it doesn't mean you'll both be eager to spend it talking on the phone or writing emails well into the night.

In this chapter, we'll explore different communication styles and discuss how conflicting communication preferences can cause challenges in long-distance dating. We'll discuss written communication and how partners can effectively express feelings via email. We'll also provide some general guidelines for communicating effectively by phone. As one woman we spoke with so aptly expressed it, "Communication is always important, but in a long-distance relationship, in many ways it's all you have. If you don't have communication, you don't have a relationship."

UNDERSTANDING COMMUNICATION STYLES

One of the first building blocks for effective communication lies in understanding the fundamental truth that people have different communication styles. How many times have you heard it said that someone is a chatterbox, or that someone else is a person of few words? Some people love to talk; others love to listen. Some of us were born with the gift of gab, while others find it difficult to find the right words in nearly any situation. Some people are eloquent writers but terrible conversationalists, whereas others are great at impromptu conversation but hopelessly lost trying to construct an email beyond a few short lines. For literal thinkers, a partner who uses sarcasm, exaggeration, or off-color humor may come off as offensive. For others, conversation without these elements is like popcorn without butter—okay enough, but not really satisfying. And time of day plays a role in determining communication styles as well. Some people are

Communication Starters

Different people have different ways they prefer to communicate, and understanding each other's preferences will allow you and your partner to set realistic expectations around communication. The following questions will help you begin to understand each other's preferred ways of communicating:

- What is your preferred mode of long-distance communication (phone, email, instant messaging, or letter writing), and why?

- What is your preferred time of day to talk by phone? Do you prefer long phone conversations with your partner or quick calls just to check in?

- Who is responsible for initiating phone calls? Should this be the role of both partners, or do job, schedule, or budget considerations make it more practical for one person to do the calling?

- Do you find instant messaging with your partner enjoyable or frustrating? If you find it frustrating, what would make it less so?

- Do you enjoy communicating by email? How often do you access your email account? Are there some topics you prefer not to discuss via email?

sharp wits in the morning but by nightfall have little to contribute. Others get a slow and groggy start to their mental processes but after dark become hooting night owls, full of ideas to share.

When we were dating, we learned the hard way that at least one of our communication preferences was quite different. Our preferred phone times conflicted, and that inevitably led to problems. One of us would start juicy discussions late in the evening, right as the other would be winding down for a good night's sleep. This difference in preference caused many a late-night argument—that is, until Chris finally explained his need to keep phone conversations light before bed. We decided to set a nine o'clock deadline for all serious conversations. If one of us wanted to talk about something important, that was fine as long as all talk wound down by the magic hour. By compromising in this way, we improved our communication and still managed to have plenty of deep discussions.

Long-distance dating provides vast opportunities for personal and interpersonal growth and development. Of course, most couples don't see the challenges they face in this way at the time they're dating. When we're living through them, problems are just problems. It's typically only after the fact that we see how we've benefited from our experience.

Moira and Anthony dated in high school before setting out for colleges in different parts of the country. Their relative inexperience in relationships—and long-distance relationships in particular—meant they had a lot to learn about successful communication. This is a common challenge for young people dating long-distance because, unlike same-city dating, long-distance dating requires a couple to master communication skills almost from the start. Without these skills, intercity relationships don't have a leg to stand on. This trial by fire was a real challenge for Moira and Anthony. Like so many young couples in this situation, they found themselves confronted with fears of infidelity, resentment about feeling tied down, feelings of homesickness, and a sense of hopelessness about the future of their relationship. While these issues can exist in any long-distance relationship, the problems are compounded if the couple has not yet developed strategies for effectively communicating difficult emotions.

Of course, long-distance dating can be a learning process even for couples with significantly more relationship experience. While they were dating in the same city, Tim and Tina didn't have any problems with communication—and then Tina started a demanding new job that took her three hours away. They had been dating locally for just over a year when the job offer came in. It seemed the perfect opportunity—too good to pass up. They had reached a crossroads in their relationship, and the distance provided the chance to see if they were cut out to be with each other long term. Nevertheless, Tina says that at the time she felt resentful of Tim for not giving up his job and moving with her. It was hard for her to understand all the reasons why Tim might want to stay behind. This put a strain on their relationship, which had been relatively stress free up to that point.

Tim says that the strong communication skills they'd developed as a same-city couple were put to the test during this initial period of separation. "The distance makes everything more difficult," he says. "You have to be understanding that the other person is experiencing the same problems, the same difficulties, as you're having with the new long-distance situation." He admits there were several times when this thinking saved the relationship. "She would call up, upset and angry that I wasn't there for her. I had to get her to understand that I wasn't ready to move yet. At the same time, it was important for me to see that it wasn't easy for her to adjust to her new life out there without me."

Understanding the communication style and, in particular, the communication time that fit you best is essential for effective communication. Likewise, understanding and respecting the communication preferences and style that fit your partner best, especially when different from your own, is an absolute necessity. For couples whose relationships started out long-distance, understanding differences in communication styles can often be a greater challenge than it is for couples whose relationships have been local at one time or another. But even couples who've dated for years in the same city can find that transitioning to a long-distance relationship presents new and surprisingly difficult challenges to communication. That's because suddenly the way they communicate is just as important as what they communicate about.

FINDING THE RIGHT WORDS

Communication is an important skill for any couple to master, of course, but its importance is dramatically increased when partners live far apart. Knowing how to choose the right words to express your feelings and needs is a vital skill for long-distance relationship success. Beyond identifying and respecting one another's preferred communication times, a long-distance couple should pay particular attention to the words they choose so as to avoid unnecessary misunderstandings. A misinterpreted joke or an ill-timed comment can far too easily sabotage phone or Internet conversations, and what may have begun as a friendly, flirtatious chat has the potential to turn into a heated argument or a hurtful exchange. Christina, a thirty-year-old accountant from Michigan whose fiancé Rick lives about seven hundred miles away, puts it well: "Communicating an idea correctly is always important, but in a long-distance dating relationship, that importance is magnified. Little misunderstandings become big obstacles."

So how do you effectively communicate ideas? For starters, try putting yourself in the other person's shoes. Knowing what you know about your partner, how will he or she likely interpret your words? What about your tone? In the event that you do say something that's misunderstood or taken in a negative light, ask yourself how your partner may have heard your statement and why it may have been likely to cause concern. By putting yourself in your partner's position, you can learn to bypass potential communication problems and successfully address minor issues before they erupt into more serious concerns.

Another important aspect of successful long-distance communication lies in remembering to stay positive and never missing an opportunity to remind one another of the reasons you're in this relationship together. Without physical closeness, emotional affirmations become much more important. More simply stated, long-distance relationships require you to say "I love you" or "You're special to me" much more frequently.

Tip: **Unless you and your partner share an equal appreciation for a particularly tongue-in-cheek style of communication, the Internet is no place for sarcasm. Before clicking "Send," check your email or instant message for potential misunderstandings. If a statement can be read more than one way, consider rewriting it, or else use emoticons— those friendly, punctuation-mark happy faces that reassure us that everything is all right.**

Mastering these skills is so important for long-distance couples because, without the immediacy and natural intimacy built from face-to-face communication, eye contact, and body language, misunderstandings are much more difficult to avoid. For many long-distance couples, differences in communication styles, if not identified and addressed, can create significant barriers to long-term relationship success. Over time, frequent misunderstandings and the subsequent arguments that tend to result can become a burden on even the strongest relationship and may ultimately lead a couple to an unfortunate breakup.

EXPRESSING DIFFICULT FEELINGS

When we first met Carla and Steven, they were dealing with communication issues that seemed to threaten the future of their relationship. For Carla, Steven was only the second man she'd dated since finalizing her divorce two years earlier. Steven, also divorced, had been on several dates since his marriage ended, but his relationship with Carla was his first truly serious foray back into the dating world.

Although both were divorced, when they met each was in a different stage of recovery from the problems that had plagued their previous relationship. To hear Steven's friends and family describe it, his marriage had been a complete disaster from start to finish. He and his ex-wife had gotten married after a very short courtship, and within a few months of marrying, Steven's wife had begun an affair with one of his friends. The problem was never resolved, and the couple divorced within a year.

Two years passed before he started dating Carla. By the time they began their relationship, he felt he'd had a lot of time to reflect upon his divorce and learn from the mistakes he'd made. With the help of close family members and friends, he'd been able to reconcile with his past and rediscover all the gifts he had to offer another person. He believed he was emotionally ready to put in the time, trust, and commitment he knew a successful, stable relationship would require.

Carla, by comparison, had been married for six years to a man she had known quite some time before deciding to marry. Friends described them as the perfect match and were shocked when news of their separation first hit. Carla herself always believed her marriage would last, and when her husband told her he wanted a divorce, it came as a total surprise. Soon after separating from her husband, she rebounded into a long-distance dating situation with a man she met on a business trip. That relationship lasted a few months, until Carla decided it was getting too serious and called it off. She still carried feelings for her ex-husband and still felt confused about why their marriage had failed. But when she met Steven, he swept her off her feet. He was confident and charming and treated her with respect and consideration, feelings she hadn't often experienced in her marriage. Steven was the kind of man friends said would be good for Carla. Even though she still felt hurt and vulnerable from her divorce, she decided to give love another go.

When we began our conversations with the couple, they had been dating in towns 150 miles apart for four months. The distance was just far enough to make it difficult to see each other throughout the week but close enough that they could date on weekends. Both Carla and Steven hoped to marry again one day and had shared this hope with one another. Both felt they had been upfront about their expectations and said they would be willing to relocate within two years if the relationship continued to flourish.

Although they believed they were on the same page in terms of goals, they still worried that certain issues remained sore spots in their relationship. Identifying those specific issues, it seemed, wasn't always easy.

One issue that was easy to spot was that each had different ideas about the ideal amount of time to spend on the phone. Once the newness of their dating relationship began to wear off, frequency of communication soon became a sore topic. Steven called Carla every night, wanting to talk for half an hour or more. He believed that this high level of frequency was important to their developing relationship. Steven also assumed that they'd spend every weekend together and regularly planned ahead for his visits.

Tip: **For many couples, cost can be a prohibitive factor for phone communication. Mobile phones offer an attractive option. If you don't have a mobile phone, we strongly recommend you consider getting one. Be sure to choose a plan that includes lots of minutes and no long-distance charges, and try to limit your talking to your free minutes whenever possible. (There is some concern that extensive cell phone use may not be safe; if that worries you, you may want to limit your time.)**

Carla told us she wanted to spend more time by herself and with family, but that she had trouble communicating to Steven her needs for time and space. And because she was still processing feelings from her divorce, she wanted to keep the relationship moving at a slow pace. Although she had said she thought she would be willing to relocate within two years, she was having second thoughts. She said it was important to her that she experience a sense of independence following her divorce. Steven, on the other hand, felt ready to move beyond his divorce and start something new. He planned to marry again someday, and thought Carla might be the one. He was eager to move their relationship forward, but she was hesitant, not yet trusting herself and her own judgment enough to know if she would be able to handle the pressure and demands of a serious relationship.

Even though they were at different stages of recovery from their respective divorces, Carla and Steven both acknowledged that they cared deeply for one another and would like to see the relationship work out. But until they could learn to effectively communicate their wants and needs to one another, relationship success didn't seem likely.

Tip: **Here's a simple, fun way to show you care: send a text message to your partner's cell phone every few days with a little love note that doesn't require any response. It's just a nice little reminder that you're thinking of your special someone.**

In order for the relationship to succeed, Steven would need to listen to and validate Carla's concerns and really try to empathize with the hesitation she was feeling. At the same time, Carla would need to understand Steven's fear that she was pushing him away. Since it had never been her intention to make him feel rejected, it was now up to her to communicate her needs clearly and in a way that would reassure him and put his fears at ease.

As it turned out, this was more easily said than done. Because Carla's divorce came as a surprise to her, she felt she had allowed herself to become too vulnerable to her husband. And because he had rejected her so plainly and without explanation, she was overly cautious about opening herself up to any more potential pain. This caution was debilitating for her in terms of expressing her feelings to anyone, particularly to a man with whom she was emotionally and romantically involved. And in a long-distance dating relationship, being closed to effective communication can often spell disaster.

Today, Steven and Carla continue to struggle with their communication issues. Carla recently told us that the whole thing has become too much for her to handle and that she's considering ending the relationship. She has never managed to express her concerns effectively to Steven, and the two have had countless arguments as a result.

Like Carla and Steven, we struggled with similar issues early on in our long-distance dating relationship. We quickly discovered that communication—expressing our own feelings and learning to listen to and respond to our partner's as well—was essential if we wanted our relationship to succeed. Unless both of us mastered those skills, we would be incapable of experiencing the kind of empathy that makes successfully relating to another person, in spite of the dividing miles, an obtainable goal. After talking with Steven and Carla, we realized that the problems threatening their relationship could have ended ours had we not learned the secrets of effective long-distance communication.

WRITTEN COMMUNICATION: A TIME-TESTED TOOL

Since it was hard for Carla to articulate her feelings in a way that made her feel heard, she and Steven might have benefited from writing letters to express their deepest feelings and needs. This is a technique we used in our dating relationship, and we've since discovered that many other couples have also put this to work successfully.

For centuries, people have recognized that letter writing is an excellent tool for long-distance communication. Letters don't have to be formal. In fact, with the prevalence of email, many long-distance couples find it easier to express their most difficult emotions in an online exchange.

Let's look at a sample email that might work to communicate difficult issues. We'll use the case of Mike and Lisa, a couple with communication problems like Carla and Steven's. In this example, Mike is writing to Lisa to express his hesitations about the speed at which their relationship is progressing.

Dear Lisa,

First off, let me express how much I care about you and that I'm enjoying getting to know you better with each passing day. I don't want to see that end.

I know I seem distant to you. Please try to bear with me and understand that this is not a reflection of my feelings toward you so much as it is the result of my own need for independence after ending my last relationship. I know you say you don't have this same need and that you're ready to move our relationship forward. Please be patient with me and give me time. I can't guarantee where this will take us, but I do care about you, and I do know that I'm willing to continue to see how it unfolds if you are. I believe I will be able to give more of myself in the months to come. I just need to keep the pace slow enough that I don't feel overwhelmed. As I've said before, I believe that if we're still happy together by this time next year, that would be sufficient time to consider moving the relationship forward and living in the same city. At this time, however, I need the chance to learn about myself and feel confident as an individual. I believe that once I know I'm a strong person in my own right, I'll be a better partner to you.

Specifically, I need to have more evenings alone where we don't talk on the phone. Sometimes I need to have an evening to myself to go to the gym or just hang out with the guys. And I would also like to cut back a bit on the number of weekends we see each other. This isn't because I don't enjoy spending time with you—I really do. It's just because I also need time to spend with my family and to get caught up on the weekly chores that pile up around here. Right now, I'm not fulfilling those needs sufficiently.

Please let me know how you feel about what I've said. I'm available if you want to talk on the phone about this tonight, and I'll also check my email if you'd prefer to respond that way. I care about you, and I'm so glad we're in this relationship together! You are special to me.

Love,

Mike

By expressing his feelings in an email, Mike is providing Lisa with ample opportunity to read and reread his points, so that she can absorb them and think about them fully before responding. Mike not only makes his point, but he does so while providing Lisa with a list of specific things he would like to see happen in response to his request. In the message, Mike asks for space but does so in a way that reassures Lisa he still wants to be involved with her. He's asserting his need for independence without alienating her or making her doubt his feelings.

KEYS TO COMMUNICATION SUCCESS

For couples preferring a more direct mode of conversation, the same points Mike makes in his email could be accomplished in a phone discussion, but it's important that each partner be willing to listen fully to the other. Before you address these sorts of issues on the phone, you may want to first write down important points and mentally go over what you hope to say, so as to be as clear as possible and not leave out anything important. Sure, there's a lot to be said for spontaneity, but when the subject matter is potentially a hot button, it never hurts to be prepared, anticipating the kinds of thoughts and feelings that your partner might experience. And don't be surprised if your partner's response is not what you expected. Part of dating is learning about one another, so it only makes sense to anticipate some surprises along the way.

Instant Messaging Do's and Don'ts

Instant messaging is an amazing tool. It's a great way to communicate, allowing for speedy communication at no expense. What could be better? If you don't already utilize this service, you can download the necessary software from Microsoft, Yahoo!, ICQ, or numerous other providers. But like any communication vehicle, there are some definite do's and don'ts that can make it more successful. Here are a few:

Do use instant messaging to chat during the workday, keeping each other posted on little daily events. This can help free up your evening phone time for more important topics.

Don't use it so much that your boss raises an eyebrow.

Do go about your own activities on the computer or even around the room while messaging.

Don't leave your partner waiting for a response while you feed the cat or water the plants. If you need to leave a conversation temporarily, be sure to let your partner know.

Do use instant messaging to talk about a wide range of topics.

Don't use it for heated or emotional discussions. When the conversation turns to something serious, splurge for a phone call.

Do use emoticons to let your partner know your intentions.

Don't expect your partner to read between the lines. Instant messaging requires direct communication.

Do give your partner a chance to respond to questions and ideas.

Don't type so quickly that your partner can't keep up.

Just springing a serious topic on your partner without warning can sometimes have disastrous results. Say, for example, you've been feeling lonely, and that's led you to have second thoughts about the relationship. Is this something you should talk about with your partner? Absolutely! Keeping your fears and insecurities secret only allows them to fester and become more powerful than they need to be. Should you drop this bombshell somewhere between asking about your partner's workday and sharing your mother's lasagna recipe? Don't even consider it. Serious topics deserve their own conversation. In this example, it would be best to either email your partner or leave a voice mail at a time when you're certain you won't get a live answer on the phone. Your initial message should be brief, direct, and sensitive to your partner's potential fears and insecurities. Here's an idea of how that initial message might go:

Hi, hon. It's me. Listen, I know we were planning on talking tonight after work. I've got something on my mind I wanted to talk to you about. Nothing terrible, but it's something I'd feel better getting off my chest. Give me a call whenever you're ready to talk. Miss you.

Notice how the message is direct about having something important to discuss without coming right out with the topic itself? Rather than leaving an insensitive message like "I'm having second thoughts about the relationship," this message simply sets the stage for the important conversation to come. As an added reassurance, the words *nothing terrible* let the recipient know a phone breakup isn't likely in the works. The phrase *give me a call whenever you're ready to talk* invites the receiving partner to initiate a call with some sense of being prepared, which can make the conversation more comfortable for both partners.

So what is the right way to have a conversation about an issue that could be painful or provoke anger? That's somewhat more complicated. There is no one right way to broach heated topics. Our suggestion is that you go over what you want to say in advance. Jot down a few notes and review and your major points mentally before talking with your partner. Be careful not to practice too much, or you'll sound insincere. The following steps provide some guidelines for thinking through tough talks with your partner:

1. **Start with the positive.** Talk about what's good in your relationship and what your hopes are for the future. (For example, "I've really had a great time getting to know you these past four months and I'm looking forward to whatever the future might bring." Or, "The two years we've been together have been amazing, and seeing how well we've managed a long-distance relationship since you moved has made me hopeful this relationship will have lasting potential.") This will help put your partner in a good frame of mind for the discussion to come and will help you reconnect with all the reasons you're in the relationship to begin with.

2. **State your concerns briefly and clearly.** ("Lately, I've found myself getting so lonely. I just don't know how I can make the distance thing continue to work much longer.")

3. **Ask your partner about his or her feelings,** and make sure your partner understands what you're saying.

4. **Propose a solution** if you have one, or ask your partner for ideas. ("I think if we're going to keep dating, I need us to make more time to be together." Or, "I'd like to keep seeing you but I don't know how to do it without losing my mind. What do you think?")

BEING A WILLING LISTENER

Above all else, remember that communication is a two-way street. As important as it can be to learn how to express difficult emotions, it may be even more important to develop good listening skills. And part of good listening means understanding how your partner typically communicates.

This was a tremendous challenge in our long-distance dating years and remains something we occasionally struggle with even today. Our families of origin often determine how we express ourselves and even how we interpret the way others express themselves. In our dating relationship, Chris often had trouble with open expressions of feeling. He grew up in a family where feelings were repressed and any expression of negative emotions or dissatisfaction was considered an attack. Kate, on the other hand, grew up in a very outspoken, expressive family. No topic had been considered taboo. As you might imagine, these differences led to some explosive arguments.

Over time, we've learned to better cope with our different communication styles. Chris has learned not to overreact to expressions of emotion. Likewise, Kate has learned to read between the lines—to hear what isn't being said as much as what is.

The best way to improve your listening skills is to make a habit of paraphrasing the important points your partner is making and repeating them back to him or her. This will not only help you with your understanding; over time it will help your partner learn better ways of expressing emotions.

The example below illustrates how a couple can use this technique in a long-distance phone call to keep the conversation from getting too heated. It *is* possible to use an argument as an opportunity to learn about each other and improve the relationship. In this example, Joe confronts Ashley about his feelings of insecurity regarding her same-city friends:

Joe: I can't stand how you stay out all night with those guys. I never know where you are or what you're up to.

Ashley: Why do you always need to know every little detail of where I am?

Joe: I don't. I just . . . I don't know. It bugs me.

Ashley: So what you're saying is that you get mad at me for going out when you're not here?

Joe: No, that's not what I mean. I just want to know where you are.

Ashley: Why, don't you trust me?

Joe: Of course I trust you. It's those guys I don't trust.

Ashley: Are you saying you don't like my friends?

Joe: No, it's not that. I guess I just feel jealous.

Ashley: Why are you jealous?

Joe: I just feel bad that I'm here alone and you're out having a good time with other people.

Ashley: So are you saying you'd feel better if I called you while I'm out sometimes?

Joe: Yeah, I guess so.

Ashley: That's not a problem. Why don't I give you a call from the club tonight?

In this example, Joe and Ashley don't avoid conflict; they use it as an opportunity to explore Joe's negative emotions and work out a compromise they can both accept.

A number of principles can contribute to long-distance relationship success, but in the course of conducting our interviews, we concluded that certain principles are especially critical to creating a lasting, committed relationship when distance and travel are factors. Effective communication is undoubtedly one of the fundamental building blocks of successful long-distance relationships. Knowing how to communicate your emotional needs, relationship fears, and innermost dreams is an important skill for anyone involved in a dating relationship. For long-distance couples, it can spell the difference between a relationship that lasts and one that quickly fizzles out.

Strong communication builds a bond and gives long-distance couples something to look forward to and enjoy between face-to-face meetings. In our own marriage, we continue to benefit from valuable lessons in communication that we learned from dating long-distance. We have learned to really listen to one another, and we understand the importance of conveying negative feelings before they fester and become real problems. Hopefully, in learning the lessons of communication your own long-distance relationship has to offer you, you will develop a deep, meaningful bond to see you through the challenges of intercity dating. With any luck, you and your partner will be practicing these skills together for many years to come.

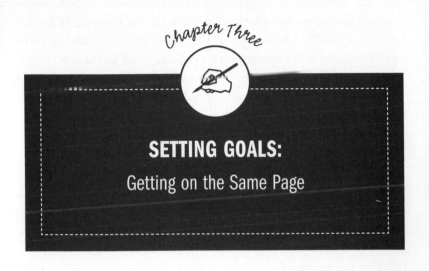

Chapter Three

SETTING GOALS:
Getting on the Same Page

As we discussed in the last chapter, among the many challenges facing long-distance couples is the potential for misunderstanding. Often misunderstandings center on the issues of independence and commitment. These issues are particularly troublesome for intercity couples because, as we've already discussed, long-distance communication is often a challenge. Then there's the added potential pitfall that the person you're dating may actually be using your long-distance relationship as an opportunity to hide from commitment. In any case, the misunderstandings many couples experience can be avoided by establishing mutual relationship goals. In this chapter, we'll talk about potential problems you might face if you and your partner aren't up front about this important process. We'll also discuss commitment and its relationship to mutual goals. Finally, we'll provide effective strategies for goal setting and time management and give you some ideas for the kinds of goals you may want to set for your long-distance relationship.

First, let's take a look at what can happen when partners don't have the same goals. David and Yolanda met at a wedding in which David was an usher and Yolanda was a bridesmaid. Seated next to each other at dinner, the two soon discovered they shared many interests and hit it off right away. David was attracted to Yolanda's fun, bubbly nature, while she found his more serious, austere personality intriguing.

Their differences extended beyond personality, however. David had established a successful, steady career in Oregon, running a local corporate recruiting firm. Yolanda, who was a few years younger, lived with her parents in central California and had floated from job to job since graduating from college. And although they didn't realize it at the time, each chose the long-distance relationship for very different reasons. For David, meeting women had seemed so difficult in his busy life that he just didn't feel he could afford to let the right one slip by. His attraction to Yolanda was so strong that, seeing the potential for a long-term connection, he was willing to start an intercity relationship. Yolanda's reasons were much more spontaneous. She liked David and thought it would be fun to date an older man. The distance, in her view, would let her keep her options open down the road.

Not surprisingly, David was anxious to see their relationship move forward. After seven months of dating, he felt the time was right to consider taking it to the next level. Since he was already well established in Oregon, he asked Yolanda to consider moving. She was applying for graduate schools with plans to attend that fall. David wanted her to consider universities near his home. He even researched a few good options and requested additional information in the hopes she would find a school that would make her happy.

But Yolanda didn't like feeling pressured to move. What she did like was living with her family in California, but even more than that, she liked the independence of not having a boyfriend nearby. "It was perfect in the beginning," she recalls. "We were both able to come and go as we liked and only see each other when the spirit moved us. When David started pushing to change things, that's when I backed away."

His view is remarkably different. "We were progressing through the relationship at a good, steady pace. Then, suddenly, everything changed. Yolanda started to withdraw, saying she wanted 'space.' Early in the relationship, we'd talked about each of us wanting to be married someday," he says now. "Why would you date someone for seven months without even considering living in the same city if your eventual goal was to find someone to settle down with?" David tried to convince Yolanda to move. When she refused, applying instead to graduate programs near her hometown, he offered to give up his self-built business and move to be near her. That's when Yolanda broke things off for good, saying David was just too serious.

So what went wrong?

Both David and Yolanda were excited about the relationship when it first began, but for very different reasons. In his late twenties, David had established his career and was looking for someone to build a life with—a goal that, in his view, could never be achieved unless one of them moved to be with the other.

Myth: Talking about the future is the kiss of death for a new relationship.

Reality: This statement probably holds more truth for same-city couples than for those dating long-distance, since local relationships provide couples ample opportunity for a gradual exploration of life goals. While we agree that pressuring your dating partner to make a serious commitment early in a dating relationship is a terrible idea, talking up front about your views on commitment and your hopes for the future is one of the best assurances you can give yourself and your partner that you're both starting out on the same page.

At twenty-three Yolanda, on the other hand, was enjoying her newfound freedom following college graduation. She saw a long-distance relationship as a great opportunity to have fun dating a special person, unencumbered by expectations of commitment or planning for the future. Early in their dating, the two had talked in vague terms about eventually wanting to find a spouse and settle down. What was never made clear was that, for David, finding a relationship with long-term potential was a *goal*. For Yolanda, it was a thought she'd entertain from time to time, but only as a pleasant daydream, not as part of any concrete plan—and certainly not as something she'd be willing to consider for at least another few years.

How could two people with such different intentions end up dating for so long? The answer is simple. Since long-distance dating doesn't allow for daily, face-to-face interactions, it's easy to misunderstand your partner's intentions. In this case, David had viewed each visit as a chance to grow closer to commitment, while Yolanda saw their weekends together as fun, wild escapes.

Because they never established clear, mutual goals for the long-distance relationship, David and Yolanda were setting themselves up for heartache. If David had made it clear early on that he hoped their relationship would grow into something more serious, Yolanda would have understood his expectations. And had she been totally honest during their conversations, she would have explained to him that, while marriage was an appealing idea to her, she knew she wouldn't be interested in establishing a serious relationship for another few years, if ever. The two might not have continued dating, and as with any breakup, the initial decision would have been difficult. But, on the other hand, prolonged heartache could have been avoided on both fronts—and David would have been free to pursue other women who may have given him the commitment he was searching for.

TALKING ABOUT GOALS

How do you know if your partner has the same goals as you? It's simple: You ask.

Many people avoid asking those questions early in a dating relationship because they don't want to appear desperate or as if they're pushing things forward too eagerly. If handled smoothly, however, such questions can help form the cornerstone of good communication in your long-distance relationship.

In David's opinion, he had asked. After dating for two months, he told Yolanda that he enjoyed spending time with her. Then he asked if she could envision their relationship ever developing into something more long-term. She said yes. In a later conversation, he asked her if she ever saw herself getting married. Again, she said yes.

He thought this meant Yolanda was interested in developing a long-term relationship with him, possibly even marrying him if their relationship continued to go well. And for David, a long-term relationship naturally implied they would live in the same city.

In Yolanda's view, she had been completely honest with David. In truth, she could have envisioned dating him for a long time, as long as they had retained the status quo of their long-distance relationship. And she did envision herself married, but not for many years down the road, and not necessarily to him.

The problem Yolanda and David faced is one that many long-distance couples must deal with—unclear goals. Neither one knew exactly what the other meant, but both went with the assumption that they were in agreement regarding the terms of their relationship. This problem could have been avoided. After dating for a few weeks, David might have said something along these lines: "I'm enjoying the time I spend with you, although I wouldn't want to continue long-distance dating forever. If we're still going strong a year from now, I would want one of us to consider moving so that we can try this relationship in the same town. Is that what you're thinking, too?"

Tip: **It's a good idea to discuss the status of your relationship from time to time, but not so frequently that you stop enjoying it along the way.**

If Yolanda had agreed, he could have then set up a "check point" to talk about the issue again, and to begin to establish a timeline for being together. He might have said something like, "Let's agree to talk again in a month and see if we still feel like that idea is worth pursuing."

After a couple of months of dating, David and Yolanda would each have had a pretty good idea of what they wanted out of the relationship. Since he was interested in reaching a deeper level of commitment, at this point David might have tried to nail down a time frame for moving the relationship forward. To that end, he might have said something like this: "I like how our relationship is progressing. If we still like where we're heading six months from now, let's start making plans to live in the same town. Would you be open to considering the possibility of moving here?"

By being direct about his goals, David would have left no room for misunderstanding. He would have stated his intention and his hoped-for time frame up front. Yolanda likely would have told him she wasn't willing to make that kind of commitment, and at that point David could have decided if he wanted to pursue the relationship with her or not, knowing that it was not likely to progress at the pace he desired. They may have ended the relationship, but at least it could have saved them some pain down the road.

A direct inquiry asking specifically what the other person is—or is not—willing to consider is more apt to elicit an honest response than a vague suggestion is. Additionally, having a specific, agreed-upon time frame is important for successful goal setting in a long-distance relationship. Both parties need to know exactly how long each is willing to keep the relationship long-distance before making a commitment to be together.

Obviously, there's a fine line between being direct and being demanding. You should never use a first date as an opportunity to tell someone that you're only interested in dating if the intention is to get married within six months, move in together in a nice little house next door to your mother, and have 1.5 children before your second anniversary. If you do that, you won't likely be getting a second date, even if that person might have been interested in that lifestyle eventually. That said, you can still avoid investing a lot of time in a dead-end relationship if both partners are honest and direct about their expectations from the start. Setting a timeline for transitioning a relationship to the same city can be an important factor in determining whether or not both parties are of a like mind.

Tip: **A word to the wise: Many people with commitment fears gravitate toward long-distance relationships because they generally don't evolve as quickly as local relationships and may continue for quite some time without ever leading to commitment.**

Of course, the kinds of goals you set for your relationship will vary depending on your age as well as whether or not you and your partner have dated in the same city for any significant length of time prior to dating long-distance. A college couple who met on spring break but attend schools in different states may initially set goals for visiting each other over summer vacation, for instance. On the other hand, a couple who dated locally for eight months prior to one partner's transfer to a new city may set the goal of dating long-distance for a year before determining whether or not they want to get married. These are just two examples of the wide range of goals long-distance couples may establish. In the end, it isn't so much the specific goal that matters; rather, it's a couple's agreement on that goal and their mutual commitment to seeing it through.

COMMITTING TO EACH STAGE OF YOUR LONG-DISTANCE RELATIONSHIP

It doesn't take a rocket scientist to know that successful relationships require work. After that first stage of a relationship in which the person we're involved with seemingly has no faults, the luster of initial attraction finally wears off and the real work of the relationship begins. You may find yourself losing patience, digging in your heels where you once compromised freely. This doesn't mean the romance is dead—it simply means the relationship is changing. With the right attitude, those changes can help you and your partner move your relationship to a new and deeper level.

That's not to say dating should be all work and no play. But having a good relationship depends on building a strong foundation, and the basis of that foundation must be a firm commitment to the relationship and to one another. When both partners care passionately about the success of their relationship, it naturally has much better odds of surviving; and consequently, the chances are better that both partners will have fun along the way.

For long-distance partners, the work of commitment becomes even more important, because long-distance dating is, at its essence, more complicated and difficult than same-city dating. When your partner is far away, even the most basic aspects of maintaining the relationship can seem to bring about insurmountable difficulties. Just finding time to see one another can be a Herculean task. And larger issues, such as fidelity and emotional availability, can become much more complicated when distance necessitates a less-frequent dating arrangement. That's why sharing mutual goals is so vital to long-distance dating success.

If you're the type who runs the other way upon hearing the word *commitment*, don't put on your running shoes just yet. Like love, commitment builds across a broad spectrum. We don't believe you need to plan your wedding on the first date. In fact, rushing into a long-term commitment like marriage can be a very foolish—and costly—mistake. Long-distance dating partners have enough difficulties to contend with without having to deal with that kind of stress. Just like same-city dating relationships, long-distance relationships require time to grow, and time for their commitment to strengthen and deepen naturally. Forcing a relationship to the next level before both partners are ready is a good way to bring it to a sure and sudden end.

But that doesn't mean you cannot or should not set appropriate goals at every stage of a growing relationship. You must. Setting mutual goals at this early dating stage doesn't mean committing to marriage or committing for life—it simply means that you recognize the work that your relationship requires, and that you promise to work with your partner to give the relationship the best possible chance for success.

To fully explore this idea, think about the natural progression of any relationship. In the beginning, you use your time to get to know one another, ask questions, and go on dates. Later, you begin integrating into one another's lives, learning more about each other and testing the water for a potential future together. Eventually, if all goes well, your relationship will likely go to the next level—marriage—the ultimate goal of most people involved in dating relationships. In many relationships, one or both partners come to the realization that a mutual goal of marriage is not in the cards and the relationship comes to a healthy end, making way for new opportunities for both individuals. Those are the stages through which most healthy romantic relationships must travel, and they're equally important if you and your partner are dating long-distance.

Let's take a closer look at the appropriate kinds of goals you might want to consider at each stage of a dating relationship. In the beginning, your primary responsibility as dating partners is to learn more about each other and decide if this relationship would be good for both of you to pursue. Honesty at this stage of long-distance dating is particularly important. Dennis, a man who had been in three intercity relationships before meeting his current partner, put it this way: "Without openness and candor, it would be very difficult to get a long-distance relationship off the ground, because the amount of time you have to get to know your partner is so limited."

During the earliest weeks of dating, the most basic goal you and your partner will want to set is a goal for spending time together. In a long-distance relationship, this can be quite a challenge in and of itself. In chapter 6, we'll discuss ways to create a successful schedule for visits and travel. But for even the best strategies to work, it's essential that both partners be equally committed to making time for the relationship and working through the challenges of long-distance dating. One partner can't shoulder the burden alone. It may work for a while, but eventually that person will grow tired of the responsibility and the relationship will fall apart. To make sure you and your partner are on the same page, it's important to talk openly about your feelings and expectations around the time you'll devote to the relationship, and the impact it will have on you.

As your relationship grows, you should set goals that have even more meaning. During this phase of a relationship, appropriate goals include continuing to make time to see one another, introducing each other to your respective family and friends, and talking openly with one another about your feelings toward the relationship—positive as well as negative. Involving each other in aspects of your personal lives can be particularly challenging in a long-distance dating relationship, where the time you have to spend physically with one another is so limited. (We'll provide practical strategies for addressing this issue in chapters 6 and 7.)

After sufficient time has passed (and the amount of time can vary from couple to couple), if you're still dating, your ultimate goal will likely be marriage. Hopefully, by this stage in the relationship, both partners are fully committed and trust that the relationship's future is solid. In the case of many formerly long-distance couples we interviewed, the decision to marry is what ultimately led them to

Communication Starters

Talking to each other about your goals is an important step you must take if your relationship is to continue moving forward. Moreover, openly communicating about your attitudes toward commitment can help ensure you and your partner are on the same page and can help you avoid the pitfalls of the serial long-distance dater described in this chapter. Use the questions below to facilitate a conversation with your partner about setting mutual goals:

- Where do you see yourself in three months? Six months? A year? How about ten years? How does your current relationship fit into those plans?

- What are your plans for marriage and family? How soon do you hope to see those plans come to fruition?

- What personal goals have you established for yourself? How might these affect your dating relationship?

- What long-term goals would you like to establish for your relationship? How might these impact your personal goals?

- Which aspects of dating long-distance do you enjoy? Which do you wish you could change?

- Would you feel the same about your partner if you both lived in the same city? Why or why not?

- If the relationship goes well, would you like to see it move to the same city? If so, how soon do you hope to see that happen?

- Would you be willing to move for the sake of your relationship?

- What would you be giving up to move to your partner's city? What do you think your partner would be giving up if he or she had to move?

- What would change in your relationship if you were both living in the same city? What would stay the same?

- Realistically, can you envision yourself living in the same city as your partner and continuing the relationship you've established?

take the ultimate step of bringing their long-distance relationship to the same city. Many couples find themselves relocating as soon as talk of marriage becomes serious or as soon as their engagement is announced. Still other couples wait until the wedding or even later for one or both partners to relocate.

WHEN "INDEPENDENCE" BECOMES "THE REFUSAL TO COMMIT"

In the first chapter, we discussed how increased independence can be one of the benefits of long-distance dating. Physical distance between two partners can foster personal growth and development outside of the relationship, an advantage many individuals actually seek, either consciously or subconsciously, when entering into inter-city relationships.

For those interested primarily in creating independence within a relationship, goal setting may not seem like a priority. This can be a mistake. Even if your goal is to retain your independence, it's best to be honest and state that goal up front. Paul discovered the independence of a long-distance relationship during his time with Loretta, a relationship that lasted nearly a year. The two first met in high school, ten years before their first date. They didn't see each other again until years later, after Paul had relocated and both he and Loretta had been through divorces. Paul, who lives in Atlanta, had gone to Knoxville to visit Loretta's brother. There was a spark between Paul and Loretta that hadn't been there before, and they began dating on the weekends.

They never set out with a goal for the relationship. They talked about what the future might bring, but they didn't have a predetermined plan. Paul preferred it that way. Because it was the first relationship he'd been in since his divorce, he was a bit cautious. "I was still unsure of myself, unsure of who I was in the relationship, and so I wasn't yet ready to set goals."

From his perspective, the distance in their relationship was beneficial. "I don't know if I could have handled dating someone in the same town so soon after my divorce," he says. "Dating Loretta allowed me to ease back into the single life, and it helped my confidence too." He says he was aware of this at the time he made the decision to explore long-distance dating. "I was wary of closeness then, and that relationship provided me the built-in space I felt I needed at the time."

There's another side of the story for Paul and Loretta. After several months of weekend dating, Loretta felt it was time for them to consider being in the same city. She had a steady, high-paying job but was willing to give it up for the sake of being together. Paul feared that her doing so would be moving the relationship forward faster than he was willing to commit, so he ended the relationship. After dating Loretta, he entered directly into another long-distance relationship for many of the same reasons he had begun seeing her.

In Loretta's view, the year she dated Paul was a year wasted, time she could have spent finding "Mr. Right." To this day, she's angry that she dedicated so much time to a relationship that wasn't moving forward. Had they discussed their goals and ideals earlier on, perhaps she wouldn't have been so disappointed.

The best way to avoid becoming involved with someone who doesn't share your hopes and expectations for the relationship is to discuss your goals from the start. There's no reason to push a relationship to develop more quickly than it should, but working together to negotiate realistic goals and create effective compromises is a good way to ensure the connection you're building is a healthy one.

THE SYNDROME OF THE SERIAL LONG-DISTANCE DATER

As we discussed in the first chapter, not everyone chooses to date long-distance for the same reasons. Most long-distance couples consider the situation less than ideal, finding themselves thrown into it by chance—either due to relocation or else finding themselves inextricably drawn to someone who lives far away. Some consider the long-distance dating situation ideal. These people may seek the independence of an intercity relationship following a bad breakup or divorce. Still others simply prefer the freedom of long-distance dating, and the sense of solitude and personal identity it allows them to keep. This last example can be a healthy attitude, or it can degenerate into something potentially detrimental to the individuals involved.

Certain individuals do chronically seem to seek out long-distance relationships over other kinds of dating relationships. These people often have a series of intercity dating partners and may never settle down. They may tell themselves they are looking for commitment, but in reality, they may actually feel more secure in the freedom of a long-distance relationship and may never find themselves willing to commit.

Ben, a financial consultant, admits that he has found himself involved in more than one long-distance dating situation. He also says the independence of intercity dating played a factor in his decision to continue a relationship with a woman he was not at all serious about, a woman whose feelings for him were deeper than his feelings for her. "It was great being able to do what I wanted when I wanted," he says. "Even though I think I knew I wasn't all that serious about her, the convenience of long-distance dating was definitely a factor in continuing that relationship. I had the benefits of a girlfriend without being tied down."

Serial long-distance dating isn't limited to men. At thirty-four, Susan is successful, beautiful, vibrant, and educated. She has never married and never truly felt the urge. Now that most of her friends have families of their own, at times she feels a pang of regret that she never chose that path for herself. She would like to believe she's interested in finding someone and settling down someday, but she admits that she's "very particular" about men, and would only sacrifice the single life for someone very special. The problem, according to Susan, is that no man ever lives up to her very high expectations.

Susan, who lives in Washington, D.C., carried on her last three relationships with men in other cities. Her first long-distance relationship was with Pablo, a twenty-five-year-old sculptor who lives in Southern California. The two met when Susan, who was traveling for business, attended a gallery opening where Pablo was showing his work. After dating for three months, he told her he was considering a move to Washington, and she broke off their relationship. Later, she said she realized she wasn't ready for that sort of commitment.

Soon after breaking off her relationship with Pablo, Susan started dating Rick, an entrepreneur with a very successful business based in Indiana and the neighbor of one of her college friends. His business obligations tied him to Indiana, but he wanted Susan to consider moving to be with him. Although she was happy dating Rick long-distance, when he started talking to her more seriously about the possibility of her relocating, she broke off the relationship, telling him she simply could not bring herself to move away from the place she called home.

Susan's most recent relationship was with Eldon. Twenty-two years her senior and divorced, Eldon was a successful cardiologist in Boston when they met. Once things began heating up in their relationship, he offered to take early retirement and move down to Washington to be with her. She ended that relationship, too, saying she didn't see herself settling down with someone so much older.

Are you beginning to see a common thread in this story? Although she probably wouldn't agree with us, we think Susan seeks out long-distance dating relationships because they allow her to avoid making any real commitment. It's a pattern we found in several of the unsuccessful intercity daters we spoke with—men and women of all different backgrounds, career paths, and ages. If you've experienced two or more unsuccessful long-distance relationships in your adult dating life, you may want to ask yourself if there's a reason you're more drawn to long-distance romance than to local relationships. Is it possible you might you be avoiding long-term commitment by putting yourself in difficult relationships—relationships that have a serious handicap from the start? Or is it just that you like having a relationship but are unwilling to give up the freedom of spending the majority of your days in what is, for all intents and purposes, the single life? If you are someone who finds yourself continually involved in long-distance dating relationships, you may want to reevaluate your reasons for dating the person you're with. Even though your intercity dating situation may be working for you at the moment, if you're not being completely honest with your partner about your motives, you could be setting him or her up for serious heartache down the road.

Most of us enter into long-distance dating assuming that, over time, our relationship will have the potential to blossom into a same-city commitment. But not everyone has this in mind as an end goal. The plain truth is that there are lots of people out there who may appear to be looking for love but never seem to date anyone in the same city. These people always seem to end their relationships before an opportunity for same-city involvement exists. In some cases, they may choose always to date long-distance and do so, admittedly or not, because they enjoy the freedom. This is only a problem if both partners are not of the same mind-set. If you choose long-distance relationships because of the freedom they allow, it's up to you to be honest with your partner and make sure that person understands your feelings on the matter. If you know already that you aren't interested in eventually transitioning to a same-city relationship, it's your responsibility to be up front.

Likewise, if you are interested in something with long-term potential but suspect your partner may have different motives, you owe it to yourself to ask. What clues should you look for? To start, take a close look at his or her dating history. If you're involved in an intercity relationship with someone who's had a series of similar relationships, take heed. That history of dead-end long-distance dating experiences could be a telltale sign of a deeper problem. Generally speaking, these people will resist setting goals and may tell you you're getting too serious when you talk about establishing mutual goals for the relationship. If this sounds familiar, then don't be surprised when you find yourself just one in a long string of love affairs. If you're not looking for long-term commitment, then by all means enjoy the whirlwind romance you are almost sure to have. But if you're looking for something stable, a person with a long history of failed long-distance romances may not be the partner for you. After all, an unresolved fear of commitment is usually the kiss of death for any relationship. In the case of a long-distance relationship, that death can be a slow and painful one.

The cold, hard truth of the matter is that if someone is unwilling, unready, or unable to commit to setting mutual goals, the subject will likely get them running in the other direction. Does this mean you shouldn't bring it up? We don't think so. If you feel strongly about how you'd like to see your relationship develop, and if you believe that enough time has passed for your partner to feel the same way, then you have a right—even a responsibility—to find out where your partner stands. If you and your partner aren't on the same page when it comes to relationship goals, it's better you find out now.

KEEPING YOUR GOALS FLEXIBLE

It's important to recognize that long-distance dating requires a greater level of flexibility than most other dating relationships. This can be particularly true when setting goals. Always remember, just because a couple determines mutual goals doesn't mean those goals can never change.

Ryan and Meagan discovered firsthand the importance of maintaining flexibility in goal setting firsthand. "He had promised me we'd be together by March. As of August, I was still waiting," says Meagan, an accountant with a Fortune 500 company. "I was really angry. I felt like I wasn't a priority in his life."

Ryan says that not only was Meagan a priority—she was his top priority. "The problem was, I knew I'd need a good job when I moved out to be with her, because careers are important to both of us and I wanted to contribute equally financially." By late August, he received an offer in Meagan's city. Within two weeks, he moved in with her and began his new job. He's grateful that Meagan stuck by him even when times were tough. In fact, he says her patience helped him see how bright their future together could be.

Shortly after moving in together, Ryan and Meagan got engaged. The couple says that having to deal with the frustrations of living in different cities for so long helped them make the decision not to postpone future commitment. "She waited for me to find a job near her. I didn't want to wait any longer at that point to commit. I knew I was ready."

A LIGHT AT THE END OF THE TUNNEL

If the thought of all this hard work has you feeling down, don't despair. For most intercity couples, mutual goals make the difficulties of long-distance dating easier to bear. Establishing a solid goal for the total length of time they were willing to spend apart was important for Deborah and Gary. "Setting a time limit to the long-distance was like a light at the end of the tunnel," Deborah says. The two met during an internship in the same city, although they were attending universities in different towns. As time wore on, they began looking at their graduation dates in terms of a "countdown." The promise of being together was a goal both could look forward to. Because they knew they ultimately wanted to be together, the challenges of dating long-distance were that much easier to deal with.

Actually, among the successful long-distance couples we interviewed, several made reference to their decision to be together and, more specifically, the establishment of a realistic target date as providing that light at the end of the proverbial tunnel. A target date and a solid commitment to live in the same city give many long-distance couples a greatly needed second wind to make it through bumpy times. Whether that target date is a month away or two years down the road, just setting a mutual goal makes the distance itself much easier to handle.

This was certainly the case for us in our own long-distance relationship. After several months of dating, the challenges of maintaining an intercity connection at times seemed just too difficult to bear. In fact, at one point the frustrations we were experiencing actually came close to breaking us up. In a heart-to-heart discussion one weekend, we came to the conclusion that if we were going to continue seeing each other, we would need to establish a target date for moving to the same city. We decided that Chris would start a job search in Cincinnati with the end goal of finding a position within four months. In reality, it was six months before we were able to be together long term, but even just knowing that it was what both of was working toward made the difficulties of living apart easier to handle. Setting a mutual goal breathed new life into our relationship and helped us make it through the homestretch.

Okay, so much planning and negotiating can seem a bit stressful—even artificial—to anyone trying a long-distance relationship for the first time. Where's the spontaneity? Where's the romance? Even though it may sound hard to believe, keeping some amount of mutual structure, goal setting, and planning in your relationship will provide the solid springboard to allow you the freedom to be spontaneous and romantic. That's because you won't have to worry constantly about your relationship's future or deal with many of the fears and uncertainties that are otherwise rampant in intercity dating. And that means you'll be free to focus on what really matters—enjoying your growing relationship.

Chapter Four

TRUST:

The Cornerstone of a Solid Relationship

Michelle and her boyfriend, Larry, met through work. At the time, she lived outside of Pittsburgh and he was in Santa Monica, but their company required both of them to travel. To help each other build trust in their growing relationship, the couple made a point of calling each other frequently and touching base by cell phone whenever either was out late at night. "Neither of us liked the checking in thing," Michelle says. "But we had to remember to keep in mind how the other would feel if they wanted and expected to talk." This was especially important on holidays and special occasions when the two were unable to be together. "We learned to say things like 'I wish you could have been there' and 'so-and-so asked about you.'" Michelle says these kinds of expressions helped each of them remember how much the other cared.

Relationships that lack a general sense of trust are often more vulnerable to the stresses of long-distance dating. Michelle says she discovered the importance of addressing the issue of trust up front with Larry. Building trust in their long-distance relationship helped them avoid potential problems and made intercity dating much easier. How do you know when trust is an issue in your relationship? According to Michelle, "It's easy to tell if you don't have trust, because you'll find yourselves fighting over little things much more."

With a solid foundation of trust, insecurities and doubts about fidelity or loyalty just don't seem to surface as often. Without that foundation, relationships get tricky. Being away from one another for long stretches of time can lead to feelings of mistrust and even resentment. Certainly this was true for Larry and Michelle. Hearing rumors of coworkers using travel as an opportunity for infidelity, each experienced their own share of suspicions. Even though these suspicions were unfounded, they began to take a toll on the relationship. "That's why trust is vital to your overall happiness as a couple," says Michelle.

Like Michelle and Larry, we faced problems caused by mistrust early on in our long-distance relationship. When we were away from one another, it was all too easy to allow our imaginations to run away from us, and before either of us knew what was happening, we were accusing one another of all sorts of imagined infidelities and untruths. Every coworker, neighbor, and friend of a friend was suspect. Many long conversations in the early months of our relationship were spent assuring one another of our faithfulness and good intentions. Our interviews with other couples confirmed our suspicion that we were far from alone in this struggle. It seemed that everywhere we looked we were meeting intercity couples who had spent long hours debating the exact same issues. The kinds of insecurities and doubts that rarely trouble healthy same-city relationships seem to be par for the course in even the best, most stable long-distance relationships.

When we initially discussed what topics we wanted to include in this book, we knew that honesty, trust, and fidelity were issues we needed to address. At first, we considered breaking them out as separate chapters. After interviewing several couples, however, the interdependence of these subjects became impossible to ignore. After all, it's only when we trust someone that it is possible to allow ourselves to open up in a completely honest way. Likewise, it's only when we're completely honest with one another that real trust can develop. And fidelity? Fidelity is a natural extension of trust and honesty; all three are equally important to the success of a long-distance relationship.

Throughout this chapter, we'll explore some of the most common problems with honesty, trust, and fidelity that long-distance couples might face. We'll provide practical suggestions for addressing these issues, including how to overcome feelings of doubt, how to deal with temptation, and how to recognize if the person you're dating is unfaithful. We'll also touch on some of the things you may want to consider if you're thinking about continuing to date a partner who's been unfaithful to you.

EFFECTIVELY DEALING WITH FEELINGS OF DOUBT

Javier and Jennifer experienced issues of mistrust when Jennifer graduated from the university where they had met. Javier, who still had a year left until graduation, stayed behind, while his girlfriend moved back home with her parents, over two hundred miles away. "It wasn't just that we were apart," Jennifer says now. "It was that Javier was surrounded by single, beautiful women who were right there, on campus and available." Her feelings of jealousy and insecurity took both of them by surprise. She says while they were in school and dating, trust had never been an issue in their relationship. It was only after she graduated that Jennifer's imagination began to run wild. As with any significant life transition, graduation can be a time fraught with insecurities. Those feelings can be compounded when a serious relationship suddenly becomes long-distance. In hindsight, Jennifer thinks it may have been her own insecurities that led her to doubt her boyfriend's fidelity. Today, they're happily married with an eighteen-month-old daughter. Still, they both remember how difficult it was to be apart, and both say trust was their greatest challenge.

In long-distance dating, as in any dating relationship, trust is a fundamental virtue. For long-distance couples, it takes on elevated importance. That's because when partners aren't in the same city, it isn't always easy to know with complete certainty what your partner is up to. Not only that, but let's face it, distance also makes it easier to cheat; and infidelity is perhaps the biggest trust-breaker there is.

So, what does real trust feel like? When it's working in a relationship, it just feels natural. In fact, trust can be as simple as a feeling of confidence that, in spite of the distance between you and your partner, you're never too far from each other's thoughts. For Jason, trusting his long-distance girlfriend, Maria, meant not getting jealous when she went out with her friends on weekend nights. While it may sound simple enough, he says this was one of the most difficult challenges in their relationship.

Jason, who was admittedly more of a homebody than Maria, would typically be home no later than ten or eleven on weekend nights. Maria, on the other hand, would often go out to a bar with friends, followed by a night of dancing at an after-hours club. Most weekends, in fact, she would stay out until three or four in the morning. Finally, after several heart-wrenching, highly charged arguments, the couple made a compromise. They agreed they both would be home no later than one in the morning on the weekends, and they would always call each other to say good night. That helped calm Jason's fears and build his trust, and it also helped Maria focus on herself as part of a couple, rather than just someone out on the singles scene. At first, phoning in was a difficult adjustment for Maria, but she recognized it was one she needed to make. "Jason was right," she says. "I wasn't single. And although that didn't mean I had to give up my social life altogether, it wasn't really appropriate for me to be out at bars and dance clubs at all hours of the night."

Tip: **If your same-city friends are the sort who like to go to bars, nightclubs, or other "pick-up spots," talk to your partner to find out how he or she feels about the matter. You may think feelings of jealousy or insecurity are unreasonable, but remember, your partner finds you attractive and knows that other people will as well.**

The late-night calls helped the couple establish trust. A quick call to say good night provided much-appreciated reassurance to Jason that he was the last person on Maria's mind at the end of the day. That one simple gesture made it a lot easier for him not to worry when she went out at night.

Learning to overcome his fears was a milestone in Jason's ability to open himself up to a trusting relationship. As he learned to trust Maria, he learned to share more and more of himself with her in emails and phone calls. The closeness between them eventually blossomed into a true and lasting love. Now that they're married,

Communication Starters

An open discussion is the first step in strengthening trust in your long-distance relationship. Remember, you and your partner may not always see eye to eye, but by understanding one another and truly caring about each other's feelings, you should be able to reach compromises that make you both happy. Here are some questions to get you started:

- Do you feel you can trust your partner fully? Why or why not?

- Do you ever feel your partner may not be telling the truth? Why or why not?

- How do you feel about the importance of fidelity in a dating relationship? How would you feel if you were to discover your partner was unfaithful?

- What was your parents' relationship like when you were growing up? Were both parents faithful? How do you think their relationship has impacted your view of fidelity and trust today?

jealousy is no longer an issue. Overcoming those insecurities early in their dating relationship ultimately enriched their connection to one another and deepened the bonds of their commitment.

Maybe you, like Jason, have experienced this sort of insecurity, or perhaps you can identify more with Maria, and your partner seems forever worried you'll have an affair. Either way, you're certainly not alone. Long-distance dating fosters relationships unlike those experienced by same-city couples. After a few lonely Saturday nights spent wishing you could be with your partner, it's all too easy to let your imagination run wild with the fear that someone else is there to take your place. More often than not, this fear is unfounded. In a same-city relationship, doubts of fidelity may likely signal a serious problem, but for intercity couples, it's not uncommon for one or both partners to worry about the possibility their partner may be unfaithful. This is particularly true when the couple has never lived in the same city, since partners who've spent at least some time dating locally will, presumably, be more familiar with each other's friends and regular routines. Still, even partners with a long history of same-city dating may be surprised when such insecurities and fears surface.

In some cases, of course, the fear that a partner may be unfaithful is well founded. The unfortunate truth of the matter is that when you're dating long-distance, you don't get to know your partner in the same way as you'd know someone you date locally, because it's harder to keep tabs on each other's day-to-day activities and whereabouts. A partner in another city can much more easily hide something from you that he or she doesn't want you to see. Sound jaded? Perhaps. But plenty of the people we interviewed for this book have been burned by not giving their trust careful consideration, or by not giving their trust sufficient time to develop naturally. Remember when we said that honesty and trust are intrinsically linked? Well, that's because trust without honesty is blind trust, and blind trust is never wise.

FACING TEMPTATION

So how do you make sure you don't give your partner any real reason to doubt your faithfulness? The best way to deal with temptation is to avoid it in the first place. If this sounds extremely simple, that's because it is. With temptations removed, fidelity is just easier. If the hottie you see at the gym every night at seven sets off fireworks, try going at five instead. If flirting with a coworker leads to thoughts of infidelity, ask yourself why you're feeling tempted. Maybe you're lonely or bored, or maybe you're insecure about your partner's level of commitment. Whatever the reason, if your relationship is important to you, our best advice is, stop flirting.

In a long-distance dating situation, it's much easier to feel tempted to stray. There are a number of reasons for this. First of all, there's the fact that if you do cheat, you probably won't be discovered. Unless your partner has an "informant" in your city who's likely to spill the beans, the chance you'll get caught cheating is pretty unlikely. Not only is it easier to get away with infidelity, but the temptation to cheat may seem more appealing. That's because when your partner is in a different city, loneliness can all too often rear its ugly head. And, like it or not, many times loneliness is a key factor in the temptation of infidelity for long-distance couples. Unlike infidelity in same-city relationships, the temptation to cheat on a long-distance partner doesn't necessarily mean there are serious problems in the relationship. Oftentimes feeling tempted may just mean you're lonely, you miss your partner, or you have insecurities of your own that have you fearing your partner could be cheating on you.

Harmon, an airline pilot who has been in two intercity relationships, says temptation to stray from a long-distance partner can be strong. He believes dating someone you don't always see on a regular basis makes the thought of cheating much more real. "It's hard to make new friends when you're on your own but not single. You end up meeting a lot of people who are interested in you."

So why not just cheat? It certainly is easy enough. It may seem obvious, but we'll say it anyway: infidelity is never a good option. The effects of cheating are far-reaching, even if your partner never finds out. When we cheat, we tear down the very foundation of honesty and trust that is so vital to a genuine relationship. Being unfaithful may feel great at first, but eventually fear and guilt take hold, and the cheater often ends up the one feeling worse for the affair. As Harmon says, "If you really want to stray, then you don't want to be in a long-distance relationship."

We're not saying you should stay in a relationship that makes you unhappy, particularly if a chance at real, lasting happiness lies just up the road. What we are saying is that if you believe you would be happier with someone local or, for that matter, anyone other than your partner, you owe it to both of you to talk about your feelings up front and discuss the possibility of seeing other people.

Tip: **Even innocent same-city friendships with people of the opposite sex can inspire feelings of doubt and insecurity in a partner who is miles away. Discuss feelings about such relationships up front and find mutually agreeable rules for both partners to follow with regard to friendships with members of the opposite sex.**

Even if you don't intend to be unfaithful, sometimes the temptation to cheat can seem overwhelming. Tamara and Steve faced that issue head-on in the course of their long-distance relationship. When Tamara joined a discussion group at the local bookstore, she wasn't looking for temptation. Nevertheless, it presented itself in the form of Anthony, a smart, sophisticated single man she met there. He was witty, sexy, intelligent, charming, and interested in many of the same things Tamara was interested in. Most appealing of all, he was local.

"When Steve was near, there was no contest. My heart belonged to him one hundred percent," Tamara recalls. "It was during those long breaks between visits that I'd start to forget how great it felt to be together. It was easy to imagine I might be happier with someone else." When loneliness sets in, many of us, like Tamara, find ourselves forgetting the reasons we were drawn to our long-distance partner in the first place. In Tamara's case, her temptation came from a simple longing for companionship. "At times," she says now, "the grass may have seemed greener on the other side, but it was always Steve I loved."

Tamara says that at first she wasn't honest with herself about her feelings. She told herself she was merely developing an innocent friendship with the other man. They exchanged emails, initially to discuss the books they were reading in their group, but after a while the conversations got more personal. Tamara found herself opening up about her relationship with Steve, among other things. Nothing about her exchanges with Anthony was outwardly inappropriate, but the level of emotional intimacy was, in some way, a betrayal of her connection to Steve. Tamara says that's what opened her up to potential trouble. "One night after the weekly group meeting, he asked me out for coffee. I said yes, and when he walked me to my car, he leaned in for a good night kiss. I kissed him quickly on the

Reality Check

Myth: When you truly love someone, you won't feel tempted to stray from your relationship.

Reality: Real love doesn't mean you don't feel tempted. What it does mean is that you care enough about your partner and the relationship not to give in to temptation, and to make every effort to avoid it when you can.

cheek and felt horrible about it. I drove straight home and called Steve to tell him what happened and to let him know I loved him."

Steve says he was hurt by her admission but glad that she was honest with him. Hearing his girlfriend describe how special another man could make her feel was really upsetting. He reminded Tamara of how much he loved her and assured her that one day they would be in the same city and then he could make her feel special every day for the rest of their lives.

It was up to Tamara to make the decision to avoid temptation. Ultimately, she decided to remove herself from the opportunity to cheat. As much as she enjoyed the social interaction of her discussion group, she decided the best thing for her relationship would be to stop attending the meetings. She also stopped emailing Anthony and explained to him that she wasn't comfortable with the direction the friendship had gone. He tried to reconnect with her a few times, but because she didn't want to take any more chances with her relationship, or to lead him on, she decided it was best to not respond.

UNFAITHFULLY YOURS

In a perfect world, everyone would be as cautious about avoiding infidelity as Tamara. Unfortunately, this world is far from perfect, and many long-distance couples don't fare as well when it comes to the issue of fidelity.

As we've said, infidelity is often a greater threat to couples dating long-distance because—like it or not—it's easier to cheat on a partner who lives far away. Denise, a social worker living in a Philadelphia suburb, learned this lesson the hard way when her boyfriend of two years, Martin, accepted a job in Detroit. When she agreed to continue the relationship long-distance, Denise's boyfriend began seeing another woman in secret.

Communication Starters

As difficult as it is, discussing temptation openly is the best way to ensure that you and your partner don't give in to it. These questions will give you a starting point for opening up a conversation with your partner:

• Have you ever felt tempted to stray from your relationship? If so, what was appealing about the idea? Did you follow through on it?

• If you have been faithful, what keeps you from giving in to temptation?

• Have you ever been involved in a relationship in which fidelity was an issue? What happened? How did it impact your approach toward relationships now?

• Does your current relationship fulfill your needs for companionship and closeness? What creative ways can you and your partner come up with to bring you closer together, in spite of the miles that keep you apart?

• When do you feel most lonely in the relationship? Is there anything you or your partner can do to lessen those feelings of loneliness?

In hindsight, she says it's easy to see how this might have happened. Martin's new job required a lot of travel, and that gave him many opportunities to meet people and form relationships without the risk that Denise would find out. For two months, she was unaware that there was another woman in his life. Then Denise decided to surprise him with an unexpected visit one weekend—but as it turns out, the bigger surprise was in store for her. In a scene right out of a Hollywood script, Denise rang the doorbell of Martin's Detroit apartment and a young woman answered—a woman who seemed just as surprised to learn about Denise as Denise was to learn about her.

We'd like to tell you that this story had a happy ending, but the situation was devastating for Denise. As it turns out, the woman who had answered the door was also involved in a long-distance relationship with their mutual boyfriend, Martin. Denise caught the next plane home, sure that the relationship was over. For weeks, Martin called her, begging her to take him back. He sent her flowers, wrote her poems, and said all the right things. Much to our surprise, she ultimately decided to take him back.

The old saying "Once bitten, twice shy" did not hold true for Denise. She threw herself back into the relationship with enthusiasm, determined to make it work. She believed that since trust is essential to successful relationships, it was her duty to trust him no matter what. What she didn't realize was that although trust is an important aspect of any successful relationship, blind trust would ultimately lead to heartache. And it did. In fact, Denise's heart was broken months later when she discovered that once again Martin was secretly carrying on relationships with two other girlfriends in two other cities. He truly had "a girl in every port."

Denise just didn't know when enough really was enough, and her determination to make the relationship work only resulted in her heart being crushed time and time again by this man. It seems Martin suffered from the syndrome of the perpetually unfaithful. And he's not the only one out there. In all our interviews, it became quite clear that this type of individual plagues the long-distance dating scene. And it isn't always the man who's unfaithful.

Ten Signs Your Partner Might Be Unfaithful

We can't tell you for certain whether or not you're the victim of infidelity, but there are some clear warning signs that may point in that direction. Here are just a few to watch out for:

1. **Defensiveness.** When you ask your partner where he's been or what she's been doing, a defensive response could indicate your partner has something to hide.

2. **Secretiveness.** If your partner seems to have a lot of secrets, one of those secrets just may be the one you don't want to hear.

3. **Limited availability.** If it seems as though your partner is always too busy with work or school or other commitments to make time for you, he or she just may be making time for someone else. At the very least, this sort of unavailability could indicate that your partner isn't interested enough in your relationship to give it the time and attention it deserves. Our advice? Move on.

4. **Friends or family you never meet.** A faithful partner will have no trouble introducing you to family and friends, because your relationship isn't something to hide. Hesitation to introduce you to the other people in his or her life usually indicates that either there is uncertainty as to whether or not you are "the one," or else someone else may already be in the picture.

5. **New friends.** Just because your partner starts hanging out with a new crowd doesn't mean that infidelity is in the cards, but don't rule it out. Many people start socializing with new groups of friends when their behavior would be frowned upon by their usual social circle.

6. **Mysterious phone calls.** A quickly dismissed call while you're around might be an attempt to hide another relationship.

7. **Strange behavior on the phone.** If your partner seems hesitant to call you by name or is too busy to talk on the phone, it might indicate that someone else is in the room.

8. **A sudden interest in seeing other people.** If your partner suddenly starts talking about how it might be time to consider no longer dating exclusively, there's a good chance he or she may already not be.

9. **Guilty behavior.** Sometimes those little surprises—a bouquet sent to the office, a romantic gift or card—may be purchased to help clear a guilty conscience. Don't jump to conclusions. A thoughtful gesture may be just that—a thoughtful gesture. But if that gesture comes on the coattails of other strange behaviors, be cautious.

10. **A gut feeling that something isn't right.** More than anything else, when it comes to detecting infidelity you need to trust your instincts. Avoid overreacting or looking for problems that aren't there, but if you don't feel right in the relationship, your best bet is to talk to your partner about your feelings and find out if they're well founded or not.

Take the example of Tracy, a forty-something divorcée who frequently dates long-distance. She admits that she seeks out long-distance relationships for the "freedom" they allow her. But what Tracy is talking about is not the kind of independence we discussed as healthy earlier in this book. She is what we call a "chronic long-distance dater." Her past three boyfriends all lived in distant cities. Worst of all, she admits that she strayed from each of her long-distance relationships, but she doesn't see this as a problem. When it comes to infidelity, Tracy's attitude is, "As long as no one finds out, then no one gets hurt."

Our feeling is that there are always victims, regardless of whether or not the infidelity is discovered. When we aren't faithful to our dating partner, we cheat ourselves out of ever really knowing just what could develop in a committed, honest relationship. A part of us is always hidden, and that means we can never truly build a meaningful, full connection. Any way you look at it, when a partner is unfaithful, nobody wins.

This isn't to say it's impossible to move past infidelities in a relationship or to make things work after an affair. Some couples we spoke with felt that surviving an infidelity actually made their relationship stronger. But one popular philosophy states, "Once a cheater, always a cheater." Surely, no stereotype is true in every case. But if your partner has cheated on you, be careful. Someone who's been unfaithful once may be more likely to have subsequent affairs, particularly if he or she feels that there are no real consequences for having been unfaithful.

After his long-distance girlfriend of ten months was unfaithful, Tyler decided to continue working on the relationship. Tyler admits that his faith in the relationship was shaken when he discovered that Dana had cheated on him. Initially he broke up with her, but eventually the two reconciled. He says learning to trust her again has been a gradual process, one that's been anything but easy. And while he says he feels like he's forgiven her, he can't forget what happened and is always haunted by the idea that it will happen again. He doesn't believe it will ever be possible to regain the level of trust that once existed in their relationship. He's forever on his guard, saying, "If I ever thought that she had cheated on me again, I would definitely end the relationship."

We think this sort of ambivalence is the unfortunate aftermath of a situation that could have been avoided entirely if both partners had been honest with one another from the start. Settling for a relationship where trust is not fully possible compromises the love and commitment all of us deserve in life. If your partner has been unfaithful, it's up to you to choose whether or not to continue the relationship. We can't make that decision for you, but one thing we will say is that neither of us would have wanted to stay with someone we couldn't fully trust. Whatever you decide, we urge you to think long and hard about the kind of love you deserve and about what you want out of a relationship, and if those ideals will ever be fully possible now that your trust has been broken.

So what should you do if you think your partner might be cheating on you? This is a potentially explosive topic, and approaching it too aggressively could lead to an unnecessary and unhappy conclusion. Likewise, tiptoeing around the subject will only suppress your fears and make them that much more powerful. Plus, if you don't address the matter effectively and it turns out your partner really is cheating, you could end up staying in a dead-end relationship much longer than necessary.

If you have reason to suspect your partner has been unfaithful, we recommend you use the suggestions from chapter 2 for discussing difficult topics with your partner. Call or email in advance to let your partner know you have something important you need to address, and set a time for the conversation. As difficult as it may seem, don't allow yourself to sound accusatory unless you have solid evidence that your partner has been carrying on an affair (incriminating photos, for instance, or a call from the other person involved). If all you have is a sneaking suspicion, this is not grounds for launching into an accusation. It is, however, sufficient reason to have a heart-to-heart talk with your partner and directly address your fears.

Here's one example of a respectful, nonaccusatory way to begin this sort of discussion:

> I care about you and I'm glad we're in this relationship together.
> Sometimes the distance between us makes it hard for me to
> believe I know where I stand in your life. Recently, a few things
> have made me wonder if there might be someone else you're
> interested in.

In this sort of communication, it's very important for the speaker to maintain a calm, matter-of-fact tone. If the other person gets defensive, it may be a sign that the speaker's fears are well founded. Regardless, the next step would be to state, calmly and without accusation, the specific things that have been the basis for the doubts. The conversation might go something like this:

> Last weekend, when I asked why you didn't call me back, you
> said you were busy with work; but the week before you said you
> had a light workweek ahead. And the last time I came to visit,
> there was that message on your answering machine from that
> person you said was a colleague, but the voice sounded really
> familiar, like someone who calls all the time. You've never given
> me reason to suspect you were unfaithful in the past, but I
> wanted to ask you about it.

At this point in the conversation, it might be best to stop talking and give your partner a chance to explain. As long as you've stayed calm and respectful, your partner should follow suit—unless, that is, he or she has something to hide.

OPENING YOURSELF UP TO THE POSSIBILITIES OF LOVE

Keeping an open, trusting relationship while making sure not to fall victim to an unfaithful partner is a delicate balance when you're dating long-distance. Fortunately, there are some practical strategies you can use to help you avoid infidelity and other forms of dishonesty. The key lies in clear and nonjudgmental communication.

Pay close attention to what we're saying here: Clear and nonjudgmental communication requires a willingness to share openly and to listen without placing blame. If you experience feelings of insecurity or dissatisfaction with your relationship, you owe it to your partner to express those feelings calmly and in the spirit of problem solving. Likewise, if your partner expresses dissatisfaction or insecurity to you, you owe it to the relationship to hear him or her out without getting defensive or placing blame.

Sound simple? Unless you're much better at communication than we were—or than most of the people we interviewed were, for that matter—open, nondefensive communication is one of the hardest skills to master. But it's also one of the most important. It's the foundation on which a trusting, honest relationship is built. Nothing is more necessary for the success of a relationship, long-distance or otherwise, than positive communication skills.

The benefits of being open and honest are too numerous to count. For one thing, you can relax more in your relationship because you'll always know exactly where you stand. For another, you'll feel confident and secure in knowing that your partner truly understands

Keeping a Relationship Journal

Being honest with yourself is the first step in achieving real openness with another person. A journal can help you reach that goal. Writing in a journal doesn't have to be a formal process. Try buying a simple notebook and recording your thoughts and feelings every day. Address issues such as how you feel about your relationship and, perhaps more importantly, how you feel about yourself. You'll be amazed by what you learn. Whether or not you choose to share your journal with your partner is up to you, but don't limit what you write about with the idea that you have to let anyone else read what's inside. Remember, the goal is self-realization through total honesty, and anything that keeps you from feeling free to be completely truthful with yourself would be counterproductive.

you and loves you no less for it. In our interviews, we encountered couple after couple whose relationships had been sabotaged by infidelity and suspicion. Keeping secrets from one another may at first seem like a good way to spare feelings or keep one another from being hurt, but ultimately it deprives your partner of knowing and loving the real you. It may be scary, but revealing your true self to someone else is the clearest, most secure path to love.

Chapter Five

CREATIVITY:

Discovering the Playful Side of Love

The playwright Rose Franken said, "Anyone can be passionate, but it takes real lovers to be silly." When we were dating, we kept this saying near our computers as a reminder while we worked . . . and while we emailed back and forth with each other througout the day. We tried to remind ourselves of this sentiment because even then we knew the success of our long-distance relationship depended significantly on how much pleasure we could derive from it and how many ways we could find to enjoy ourselves, even through the hardships of intercity dating.

Taking time out for fun is important in any relationship, but it's especially so in long-distance relationships, when everyday pressures can seem so overwhelming. Sometimes a little childlike play is just the thing you need to help build intimacy, relieve stress, and express affection. Successful intercity couples often find themselves doing things they've not done since their very first dating experiences, in junior high or high school. They write giddy love notes; they keep favorite photos on their nightstands; they send homemade cards and presents. This willingness to be creative and connect in playful, affectionate ways has helped many couples build stronger bonds while effectively expressing their feelings for one another.

Trisha, a thirty-four-year-old businesswoman from Rhode Island, says making little presents for her boyfriend Randy helped her connect with him. A compilation CD Trisha made him became one of Randy's favorites in his collection. Trisha says that even though it was a small gesture, Randy really appreciated it, and it made her feel good to know she'd done something to boost his mood and help him feel closer to her.

Creativity is essential to long-distance dating, but unfortunately it's too often overlooked. Ideas about what an adult relationship should be can keep us trapped within the confines of our inhibitions. But to achieve real intimacy, it's critical that we open up and share even the most playful and impulsive expressions of who we are. This is especially important for achieving closeness in a long-distance relationship, where the smallest problems can take on seemingly serious proportions. It takes a good sense of fun and humor to balance out the sometimes overwhelming pressures of long-distance dating.

In this chapter, we'll explore a wide range of opportunities for creative expression. We'll share ideas that worked for other couples,

The Top Ten Love Songs to Send a Long-Distance Partner

Today's technology makes It easy to download favorite love songs and burn a CD for your partner. Here are our suggestions for some classics that really go the distance:

1. "Working My Way Back to You," The Spinners

2. "Please Mister Postman," The Beatles

3. "I'm Gonna Be (500 Miles)," The Proclaimers

4. "Skylark," Ella Fitzgerald

5. "Leaving on a Jet Plane," John Denver

6. "Friday I'm in Love," The Cure (this one's good for all you weekend travelers)

7. "Reach Out, I'll Be There," The Four Tops

8. "I'll Be Seeing You," Frank Sinatra

9. "You'll Be in My Heart," Phil Collins

10. "Somewhere Out There," Linda Ronstadt and James Ingram

to inspire you to take your long-distance relationship to a whole new level. Many of these ideas involve using the Internet. If you're not computer savvy, now is the time to learn. There is no better tool for building a successful long-distance relationship than the Internet. It's no wonder that in this age of instantaneous communication, more people are venturing out into the world of long-distance dating.

For many of the couples we've spoken to, this one single tool has been largely responsible for the success—and in many cases, the very existence—of their relationship. Whether you decide to go the Internet path or choose more traditional means of communication, we encourage you to open up to the idea of being spontaneous—romance is supposed to be fun. You'll be surprised how a little creativity can help you build a stronger bond.

MOM WAS RIGHT: WHY THE BEST GIFTS REALLY ARE HOMEMADE

Jenny and Ray, a newly engaged couple, discovered the importance of creativity when Ray, an army officer, was called to duty in the Middle East. Like many partners of troops overseas, Jenny sent letters almost daily. But she also sent fun homemade cards to cheer him up. Ray says the letters and cards made him feel especially close to his fiancée during the lonely nights away. One foldout card made of construction paper hearts arrived on a particularly difficult day. On each heart, Jenny had written a different thing she loved about him. On the last heart, she wrote, "Near or far, I'm so glad you're mine to love." Ray says that card really helped his outlook. It reassured him of Jenny's love, and that raised his spirits.

Email has made written communication much more immediate, but don't undervalue the impact of a hand-written card or letter. There's something special about receiving a love letter or even just a brief note. A letter, card, or package reflects the time and care spent in sending it. And a little bit of time and some creative thinking go a long way in letting someone know you care.

Creating something special for your partner serves two valuable purposes. First, the time you spend planning and putting together a care package, card, or gift allows you to fully experience your feelings for the other person by focusing your energy on doing something thoughtful for him or her. Second, the item you create will help your partner feel loved and cherished. As an adult, you may feel foolish buying construction paper and crayons, but don't let that stop you. Many times, the more whimsical the present, the better its effect.

Carrie and her husband Brad dated long-distance during college. Carrie says that when they were dating, Brad often sent flowers or gifts he'd buy online. But her favorite gift above all others was a little origami crane Brad had made out of wrapping paper and tucked into a card. He had told her it symbolized his everlasting love. Even now, the couple keeps it on their dresser to remind them of their commitment to one another.

Let's be honest: most of us would never dream of spending time learning how to make origami for our partner if the relationship were local. But that's one of the things that makes long-distance dating unique. Gestures like this help create intimacy, which is often quite difficult to foster in long-distance situations. Ultimately, this intimacy is the foundation stone into which the language of love can be carved.

LOVE BY MAIL

Handwritten letters can be deeply romantic and sentimental, or they can be short, simple reminders of the relationship you share. Really great letter writing is an art form. We've found that the key to writing a good letter is sincerity. Giving advanced thought to the details— such as choosing special paper or a nice, comfortable pen—can go a long way toward ensuring your letter is a good reflection of your feelings for your partner. Writing your letter by hand generally takes some time and allows you to really open up your thoughts as you write. Unless your handwriting is very difficult to read, a letter is worth ten emails any day. Still not sure where to begin? There are several books available on the subject of writing good letters, although we believe the best way is as simple as writing from the heart.

Since a letter stuffed in an envelope is pretty standard, you may want to consider dressing it up. For a little extra eye appeal, decorate the envelope with words, doodles, or sayings. (A book of famous quotations can be a good investment.) You can also add to the contents inside your letter. When we were dating, we paid attention to the everyday products in each other's apartments. We'd scan the Sunday paper and favorite magazines for coupons for those items, and then send them to one another every now and then. It was a great way to show interest in and concern for each other's day-to-day life, elements that can be challenging to create in long-distance relationships.

If your partner has moved out of town and you've remained, letters can go a long way toward helping him or her stay connected to old stomping grounds. You can regularly scan the newspaper for sports stories or articles of local interest to send. Trent, a customer support manager, told us his girlfriend Melanie started sending sports scores from local teams. Although he could have looked them up on the Internet, having the actual clippings from his hometown paper helped Trent feel more connected to home, and to Melanie.

Actually, sending newspaper and magazine clippings is a good idea even for long-distance couples who have never lived in the same city. Mailing recipes, stories, and articles that your partner might find interesting is always a thoughtful gesture. We even talked to one couple who used to send each other clippings from the opinion section of their local newspapers so they'd have something interesting to discuss later. Whether you choose to try this approach or not, keeping up with current affairs is a great way to make sure your phone conversations never get boring, and it can help ensure that you don't focus solely on the difficulties of dating long-distance.

Top Ten Tools for Creative Card Making

Here are some items you can keep together in a shoebox, crate, or other handy storage container to use in creating meaningful, memorable cards and other small, mail-friendly crafts:

1. A rhyming dictionary

2. Photographs of yourself, favorite places, or the two of you together

3. A book of quotations

4. A glue stick or rubber cement

5. Colorful cardstock (acid-free paper is best for long-term use with photographs)

6. Stickers

7. Colored pencils, markers, or crayons

8. A good pen

9. Movie ticket stubs, travel brochures, or other small, flat souvenirs of times spent together

10. A book of love poetry

Beyond clippings, inserting a piece of memorabilia from one of your dates (a movie ticket or postcard, for instance) is a sentimental way to remind your partner of good times you've shared. If that's not quite your style, a snapshot or two from your last visit can be endearing. Whatever you choose, the idea is to include a personal element that takes the letter beyond a basic communication of facts or feelings and allows partners to make a tangible connection.

Of course, these aren't the only kinds of communications couples send each other through the mail. A businessman named Mike told us he sends his long-distance girlfriend picture postcards as a visual cue to how he's feeling. Postcards are a great way to say "hello" or "I love you," and they're inexpensive, too. Their pictures can help you express whatever it is you want to communicate. Bookstores often carry unique selections with unusual subject matter. Museum gift shops are another great place to hunt for postcards. Not finding just the right image? Using a scanner and medium-weight cardstock for your printer, you can make your own. It's a quick, personal way to let your partner know he or she is on your mind. After all, a picture is worth a thousand words. A personalized postcard, perhaps with your picture or a photo of the restaurant where you had your first date on the front, is a perfect addition to your partner's refrigerator door and a great way to show you care.

A letter or postcard every week may seem like an unnecessary effort, but when you're on the receiving end, it makes a world of difference. Margot, a teacher whose boyfriend frequently sends her personal messages, agrees. "It's really touching to know that he's willing to be vulnerable with me," she says. "And sending a letter or card seems much more personal than just talking on the phone." Most couples we spoke with agreed that even small gestures like these can contribute to the success of a long-distance relationship. That's because knowing someone special is thinking of us and taking time to do things for us goes a long way toward making us feel loved.

Another way long-distance partners express their love is by sending gifts, often for no reason at all. Kent, a software company account executive whose long-distance girlfriend frequently sends flowers as impulse gifts, says that, although most people think of flowers as something for women, he loves it when his girlfriend orders them for him. "Nothing outrageous or overly girly," he says, "but just something small and subtle to remind me of her." Many contemporary florists offer bouquets designed specifically to appeal to men. If you're shopping for a man, consider strong, exotic flowers, such as birds-of-paradise. Live plant arrangements and succulents can also have a masculine touch.

When we were dating, we used to send each other the occasional bouquet. It was a great pick-me-up, particularly when the time between our visits stretched out beyond a few weeks. A surprise floral delivery is best when it's least expected. If your partner has a sweet tooth or a sentimental streak, you might want to add chocolates or a plush animal with your order. It's easy to send a flower order quickly via the phone or the Internet. We received beautiful flowers and excellent customer service from ProFlowers (www.proflowers.com), Hallmark (www.hallmark.com), and Virtual Florist (www.virtualflorist.com). (Virtual Florist also allows you to send a "virtual bouquet" in an email for free.) If you prefer to order flowers directly from a local florist in your partner's city, search the yellow pages online at www.yellowpages.com.

Flowers may not be everyone's style, but a balloon bouquet is a fun variation that just about anyone can enjoy. Florists often offer balloon bouquets, but many cities also have balloon specialty shops that cater specifically to this market. Again, www.yellowpages.com should point you in the right direction.

Vicky, a publicist, told us about a special surprise her boyfriend planned for her thirtieth birthday—a singing telegram. She and some friends were out celebrating, and her boyfriend, who had coordinated the surprise with one of Vicky's hometown friends, sent someone dressed as the Grim Reaper to the restaurant to sing "Happy Birthday." (Before going this route, consider your partner's personality and whether receiving this sort of greeting in public would be a welcome surprise . . . or grounds for a breakup!)

One of our favorite ways to show one another we cared was to send a get-well package whenever one of us was sick. Let's face it, being sick is never fun. But not being able to care for someone you love when he or she is feeling bad can seem even worse. When your partner is feeling under the weather, a well-planned care package can be just the thing to help you feel closer. It's a good way to show that you care and are wishing you could be there to help. Putting together a nice get-well package doesn't have to take a lot of time. You can send a great care package simply by visiting an online pharmacy and ordering a collection of homeopathic medicines, herbal teas, throat lozenges, and special treats to help your partner down the road to recovery. We found a good selection at www.drugstore.com, but there are many options available.

Lindsay, a real estate broker, says that when she's working long hours and dealing with a lot of stress in her life, her boyfriend, John, orders her a pizza—prepaid and ready to enjoy. The first time he did it, the pizza was a huge hit. It arrived just as Lindsay pulled into her driveway following a particularly harried day. Pizza chains often will allow you to place an order and pay online, which means you can send your partner dinner when he or she is particularly stressed or blue. This is how John was able to send Lindsay dinner prepaid. To try this yourself, visit the website of your partner's favorite pizzeria to see if it offers this option. If not, it may still be possible to pre-pay by phone. If you decide to try this, we recommend you give your partner some warning that a pizza is on the way, or the delivery person may end up getting turned away at the door by your confused boyfriend or girlfriend. That said, we think this is a fantastic idea that could help make a difficult day easier on your partner, and it will go a long way in showing you care.

Sweet Hearts for Your Sweetheart

You don't need to be a pastry chef to create this tasty surprise—you just need some premade dough, a tube of store bought icing, and a lot of love.

Purchase refrigerated sugar cookie dough, typically sold in the grocery dairy case. Look for the kind designed for use with cookie cutters. With a rolling pin, roll the dough out flat on wax paper or freezer paper spread out on your kitchen counter. Sprinkle the rolling pin with flour to prevent sticking. Use a heart-shaped cookie cutter to create the lovey-dovey cookies. (Any store specializing in kitchen items should have them in stock.) Bake according to package instructions and write out love messages using store-bought colored cake decorating icing and a writing tip. Note: Don't opt for cake decorating gels—these won't dry properly for shipping.

If possible, ship the cookies within twenty-four hours of baking. Wrap them individually in plastic wrap and pack them in an airtight container. The more tightly you pack them, the less the chances the cookies will break. Put the container in a box and surround it with shipping material such as packing paper or foam peanuts. Mark the shipping box as fragile and select the earliest delivery date your budget will allow.

Want to get even more mileage out of your efforts? Send half the cookies now and freeze the other half to send later, or share them the next time you're together. (Freeze cookies before applying icing, since icing doesn't always freeze well.)

Gifts don't have to be expensive. Bookmarks, refrigerator magnets, prayer cards, origami creations, stickers, and printed poems all mail flat and can often be sent without the need for additional postage. Some websites allow you to put your own digital photos directly onto cards, mugs, calendars, and just about anything else you can think of. A calendar made with photos taken throughout your relationship makes a terrific gift. We found a good selection of products available at Kodak EasyShare Gallery (www.kodakgallery.com), but there are many websites that offer photo-based gifts for sale. All you need is a digital camera or a scanner. If technology isn't your thing, you can take your photos or negatives to a specialty shop that creates calendars and novelty gifts made from personal photos. Not sure where to look? Try asking at your local camera shop. If they can't help you, they'll usually be able to point you in the right direction.

USING YOUR TALENTS

Bill, an engineer who also plays guitar, sent his girlfriend Margaret recordings of songs he wrote for her while they were apart. When they got together for visits, he played the songs for her in person. The gesture was a big hit. If, like Bill, you have an artistic talent, you can use it to create something truly unique. And you don't have to be an artistic genius to make an impact.

Carolyn never considered herself a poet, although she was clever at constructing light, sometimes humorous, rhymes. Occasionally, she would send her long-distance boyfriend Garrett emails with audio file attachments of her reading the short verses she had written for him. Although she admits her poems weren't always brilliant, she says Garrett saved every one. Sometimes he sent her replies in rhyme, and eventually it became their own private game. Not only did the poems provide a simple, romantic activity the couple could enjoy together; Carolyn says they also allowed her to share a side of herself with Garrett he may otherwise have never gotten to know— her sense of humor. It's one of the traits she says she likes most about herself, and sharing her poems let Garrett know that part of her much more easily than he would have only through emails and conversations on the phone.

A sense of humor is important in any relationship, but perhaps even more so in long-distance dating, since the stress of maintaining an intercity connection has the potential to drain the life out of a would-be-fun partnership. When we were dating, we used to hide silly snapshots and sticky notes with personal jokes around each other's apartments or inside one another's luggage. These little surprises would be found later, often days or weeks after a visit. Even today, this has remained a sort of tradition in our relationship, something we do now and then to brighten each other's day.

Couples who enjoy making things with their hands have found countless opportunities to create unique, special gifts. Danielle made a photo flipbook for her boyfriend Joe while he spent a semester overseas. She purchased a small scrapbook at a local craft store and put in humorous photos of herself, looking wistful and sad, alone in all the places where they used to spend the most time together. Captions underneath each photo described how lonely she was without him. On the last page, she put a photo of herself with all their friends holding a sign that read, "Come home soon, Joe!"

For an even more lifelike reminder, consider videotapes or DVDs. Luis made his girlfriend a DVD showing her the highlights of a typical day in his life. He set the camera on a tripod and kept a video diary throughout the day. Clips from the diary were interspersed with video Luis filmed as he walked through the city streets to work, to the market, and to the subway headed for home that night. The short video provided a realistic "slice-of-life" look at the things he did every day.

STRENGTHENING YOUR BOND WITH ONLINE RELATIONSHIP BUILDERS

While we prefer traditional mail for creating a sense of closeness, no one can deny that email has a distinct advantage when it comes to immediacy and ease of use. Because it's so convenient, email allows couples to have ongoing conversations on all kinds of topics. This is particularly useful if partners have trouble connecting by phone due to schedule conflicts or time zone differences.

As spontaneous as email but worlds more fun, e-cards provide yet another way couples can show they care. For a relatively small investment, several websites let you send all sorts of exciting animated e-cards to your partner. Many of these sites allow you to send the cards for free. To find out what's available, search the Internet for "electronic greetings" or "e-cards." Our favorite site for free electronic greetings is Hallmark (www.hallmark.com). For a small fee, you can also join Egreetings (www.egreetings.com). This site has lots of great animated cards and also offers some that you can send without a paid membership.

E-cards aren't the only creative way couples can express themselves online. When we were dating long-distance, we used to make up fun question-and-answer games to play over email, using questions we'd pulled from books or our own imaginations. (See the sidebar Scrapbook by Mail in this chapter for an email question game to try.) Because we had never dated in the same city, there were many things about one another we might not have learned had we not found creative ways to connect through email. These kinds of games can be useful for long-distance couples whose relationship started out in the same city, as well. One variation is for couples to guess how their partner will answer before sharing their responses.

With its vast pathways of online entertainment, knowledge, shopping, and travel, the possibilities awaiting couples on the Internet are virtually endless. When we were dating, online games were just one of the many ways we discovered the Internet could bring us closer together. To try this with your partner, first be sure you are both using some type of instant messaging tool (discussed in chapter 2). If you like, you can purchase two sets of the same gaming software as long as that software has a version for online play. But you don't have to spend money to play games online. Several websites have classic board, card, and arcade games you can play for free; check out Games.com, Yahoo! Games (http://games.yahoo.com), and Vinco Online Games (www.vogclub.com). It's an easy way to have a little fun together during the workweek, and you can communicate via instant messaging as you play. Some gaming sites do include chat tools, but if you opt to use these instead of standard instant messaging software, be warned: you may be unpleasantly surprised to discover your conversations aren't as private as you think.

Other couples have found that regular board games work nearly as well, just using instant messaging and two copies of the game board—one at each location. Vince and Becky, a couple who dated long-distance for two years before moving in together, used to make Wednesday night game night. Using their favorite trivia game, each of them kept a set of dice and a box of question cards near each of their computers. Becky would set up the game board on the floor near her desk, and the couple would communicate via instant messages to move around the board, ask and answer questions, and accumulate points. While this may not be as ideal as playing in person, we think it's a far better alternative than sitting around alone and bored.

Stephanie, a graphic designer who met her long-distance boyfriend, Will, online, discovered how easy it was to share special memories and events from her life by utilizing photo-sharing websites like Kodak EasyShare Gallery (www.kodakgallery.com), Winkflash (www.winkflash.com), and Snapfish (www.snapfish.com). These sites allow couples to create virtual photo albums online. This is easiest when working with a digital camera, but if you have a scanner, you can also scan in photos from traditional prints. In most

Scrapbook by Mail

Scrapbooks are a creative way to archive the times you and your partner have spent together. You can create "scrapbook letters" with memorabilia from your dates enclosed. Each letter becomes a page in a scrapbook of your dating relationship. Adding photos to your pages can help liven things up. Self-adhesive photo corners (available at most craft stores and other retailers of photo albums and scrapbooks) hold your photos in place without damaging the backs. If you want to get really creative, you can add stickers, quotations, and even drawings. Depending how meticulous you are, you may want to send your pages in a large, flat envelope. Adding a piece of cardboard inside the envelope will increase mailing costs, but may help keep your pages in top form. When you are together, you can put the pages together in one book, which each of you can take turns keeping. Plastic page protectors are available where scrapbooks are sold, so you can simply slip your pages into the page protectors and insert them into your book. Traditional scrapbooks are available for regular letter-size paper, so if you don't mind folding your pages, you may not even need to spend extra on postage to make this creative idea work.

cases, these sites allow you to write creative descriptions of the pictures, determine order, create slideshows, and save albums on their server for future viewing. Once you've created your online photo album, you and your partner can easily upload photos to share with one another.

Metaphorically Speaking

A fun email question-and-answer game to try is something we call "Metaphorically Speaking." In this game, both you and your partner finish a series of statements using creative metaphors to share insights into your personality, thoughts, preferences, and feelings. You can use the examples provided below or come up with your own:

If I were an animal, I would be a _____, because _____.

If I were a car, I would be a _____, because _____.

If I were a song title, I would be _____, because _____.

If I were a color, I would be _____, because _____.

If I were a famous work of art, I would be _____, because _____.

If I were a style of music, I would be _____, because _____.

If I were a place, I would be _____, because _____.

Along somewhat similar lines, a website we found useful when we were dating was MyFamily.com. This site allows you to share not only photographs, but also media clips, journal entries, polls, and other fun things. This can be especially entertaining for couples with mutual friends, since several people can participate in one "family" page. There is a fee to use the site, but if you're inclined to share lots of things over the Internet, it may be worth the investment.

VIRTUAL DATES

When we were dating, we often enjoyed Saturday night—even though we were hundreds of miles apart. We called it "virtual date night." Admittedly, our friends thought we were crazy, but for couples craving closeness, a long-distance date is better than sitting at home alone. Perhaps not surprisingly, many of the intercity couples we interviewed for this book had come to the same conclusion. Virtual dating seems to be a popular alternative for long-distance couples.

Tip: **Sometimes having a tangible reminder of your partner can help ward off loneliness during times apart. When looking for the right object, engage your senses. A sweater that holds the scent of his cologne satisfies smell and touch. A picture of her in a special frame that allows her to record a quick message includes sight and sound. The more senses you can involve, the better your chances of evoking a deep and genuine feeling.**

As long as both partners treat the planning as seriously as they would for a same-city outing, virtual dating can actually be a lot of fun. The best place to start is with an agreed-upon date and time. If the plan involves watching a movie together, both partners should arrive at their local video rental store at a predetermined hour. Using mobile phones, couples can walk through their respective rental stores and find a movie they can both rent and enjoy. In this way, it's as if they had rented one copy of the movie and were going home to watch it together. For less spontaneous types, the decision of which movie to rent can also be made over email, with each partner scanning the online New Releases section of a DVD retailer to find a movie that appeals to both. This idea also works well for partners who subscribe to an Internet video rental service. As long as the selection is made well enough in advance, the couple should be ready to go with the same movie in time for their date. (If you try this idea, you may want to consider *Sleepless in Seattle*. It's the ultimate romantic comedy for long-distance dating partners.)

For an added element, many long-distance couples figure dinner into the virtual date equation. (After all, what makes for a better date than dinner and a movie?) To try this idea with your partner, you should agree on a type of food or a general theme, such as Italian, Mexican, or vegetarian. Get a carryout order from your favorite restaurant that fits the evening's theme. Even though you're not eating in the same location, you are eating the same type of food—as if you were at the restaurant together and each ordered something different off the menu.

We used to call each other once each had the movie and carryout food at home and we were both ready to kick off the date. We would have a nice, laid-back dinner conversation, as if we were enjoying dinner at the same place. While it was somewhat tricky to eat and talk on the phone at the same time, we found it was manageable. Other couples we spoke with had made this idea work with a speakerphone or using a hands-free phone. A webcam would also be an alternative for making this work, but only if both partners have high-speed Internet access.

After dinner, we would say our good-byes, start the movie at the same time, and enjoy the show. When the DVD was over, we called back to discuss the film, chat a bit more, and wrap up our date. While we couldn't snuggle on the couch together during the movie or kiss each other good night, this simple activity did help keep us both entertained for a weekend evening and provided some much-needed closeness in our relationship.

Another memorable virtual date we shared was a bookstore scavenger hunt. This is something any long-distance couple can try. It doesn't require much more than a little imagination, some petty cash, and a trip to the bookstore. Believe it or not, that can add up to the perfect formula for an interesting Friday night spent "together," made all the more exciting when you are racing against the clock to complete a scavenger hunt. Compared to a traditional scavenger hunt, a quest in the bookstore can be more heartfelt and enlightening. Not only can you find little gifts and trinkets, you can also find all sorts of poems, funny stories, and interesting facts to share with one another. The objective here is to have fun while also taking advantage of the opportunity to share with your partner.

To try this idea out for yourself, develop a list of things to find or tasks to accomplish in a bookstore. Get creative with your list. Here are some activities you might include:

- Write down a poem that in some way moves you.

- Copy a recipe for a dish you think your partner would enjoy.

- Find a gift for under $5 (or $10 or $20, depending on your budget) to give to your partner.

- Read a chapter from a nonfiction book about relationships.

- Read a chapter from a nonfiction sex book, such as *The Kama Sutra* or *The Joy of Sex*.

- Find a love spell and read it out loud, even if other people can hear you.

- Learn some facts about a major historical event that would be of interest to your partner.

- Find a quotation that applies, in some way, to your relationship.

- Learn how to play a new game and share it with your partner.

Agree to arrive at your respective bookstores at a specific hour. Give yourself enough time to make it through your list and still enjoy yourself. You want to be speedy, but not so much so as to make it stressful. If you can't make it through your list, it's okay. The idea is to do as much as you can and share what you discover with your partner. Once you reach the end of your allotted time, contact your partner, regardless of whether or not you've found everything on the list. If you're both having fun and want to continue searching, go for it! When you're ready to leave, gather your treasures and head for home.

When you arrive home, call your partner again. Share everything you wrote down or learned, telling why you chose to read the selections you picked and what they meant to you. Take the gift that you bought and mail it to your partner, or wrap it up to give when you see each other again. The next time you see each other, prepare a meal using the recipe you found in the bookstore.

LEARNING SOMETHING NEW

One way same-city couples frequently bond is through shared activities, hobbies, or classes. If you live miles apart, chances are you won't be signing up for dance lessons together anytime soon. But there's no rule that says you can't take them while you're apart. It actually is possible—and in some ways even more rewarding— to learn a new skill as a couple when you are living in different cities.

Kendra and Ryan decided to try dance lessons in their respective towns. Kendra really wanted to learn salsa, but Ryan was more interested in swing, so they couple decided to take lessons two nights per week—salsa and swing. Each was able to find a dance school nearby that taught lessons to individuals. (If you try this idea, you'll find that most dance schools have teachers available for one-on-one instruction. Make sure you investigate all fees—sometimes there are hidden charges.) Although they would have preferred to sign up for lessons on the same nights of the week, they weren't able to; but in the end, it didn't detract from the sense of shared experience. Through the process, Kendra and Ryan not only learned something new; they also made new friends—something nearly everyone involved in long-distance relationships can appreciate. Best of all, on weekends spent together, they were able to share what they had learned and have fun strutting their stuff together.

This idea doesn't just have to be applied to dance lessons—there are plenty of things long-distance partners can learn as individuals that can be shared when they get together. If, for instance, neither you nor your partner has tried in-line skating, you could both head out to the used sporting goods store and buy yourselves skates—and helmets and knee and elbow pads, too. Then you can spend a few hours on a Saturday morning learning to get your balance and maneuver on the skates. When you're together next, you'll be able to have a fun date skating through the park.

If you're both creative types, or would like to be, you could try something artistic. Perhaps you and your partner would enjoy taking up watercolors, working with clay, or writing poetry. There are plenty of instruction books for beginners out there that can get you started. Once a week, set a date to work on your new artistic pursuit together. Then send your masterpiece off to your partner in the next day's mail, or else wait until you see each other to exchange your gifts. (In the meantime, you can snap a digital picture and email it, if you'd like.)

If you're a couple of bookworms at heart, you might enjoy your own two-person book club. Read the same book and discuss it over email or your instant messaging tool. History buffs might enjoy reading up on a subject or event of interest to both partners and then sharing what each has learned. This is a great way to develop an intellectual connection.

That brings us to an important point. Don't underestimate the value of developing an intellectual bond. It's important to learn how your partner thinks and to understand the kinds of ideas that spark his or her interest. Sometimes it's difficult to understand another person's thinking, even when you see that person every day. It is doubly challenging when you live far apart. So take up an intellectual pursuit together. It's fun!

Tip: **If you and your partner regularly visit each other, why not plan occasional visits in unusual destinations? When we lived in Ohio and South Carolina, respectively, we often met up in a small town in Tennessee because it made the trip considerably shorter for both of us. You can meet for more exciting adventures as well. White-water rafting, camping, extreme sports, vacation tours, and volunteer or service trips can all be booked in advance and shared by adventurous partners. Check with a local travel agent for ideas.**

The risk of looking foolish may make it hard to open up, but creativity and a sense of humor are essential elements for the success of any dating relationship, particularly one that takes place over so many miles. In our own long-distance relationship, playful creativity was often the one saving grace that kept us from going out of our minds with loneliness and boredom during particularly long stretches apart. In the end, our intercity dating experience has helped us keep our relationship full of romance and spontaneity, even today. It's all too easy for same-city couples to get caught up in the monotony of daily life together. Should you decide to take your relationship to the next level, learning to be creative will help keep the spark of romance alive for years to come. We hope the ideas here get you started on your own long-distance romantic adventures. The only limit is your own imagination.

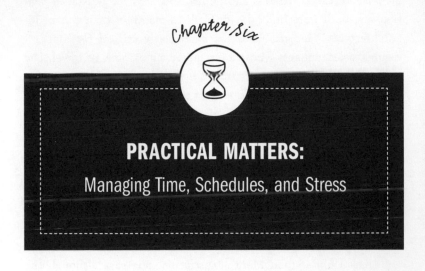

Chapter Six

PRACTICAL MATTERS:
Managing Time, Schedules, and Stress

Sometimes attraction, flexibility, and communication aren't enough to keep a long-distance relationship afloat, even when two partners care for each other. Commitment is another key piece of the puzzle. In long-distance dating situations, commitment is particularly critical to relationship success, as it is the foundation for establishing effective time management. And without effective time management, the effort required to sustain a long-distance relationship can seem insurmountable.

Take the example of Sharon and Mark. Between juggling the demands of career, friends and family, and their long-distance relationship, both were finding it difficult to maintain their independent lifestyles. This problem was particularly critical for Mark, a regional sales manager whose job required a great deal of travel. The two had been dating successfully for seven months, but in their eighth month together, Mark decided to call it off. He loved Sharon, but the stress of long-distance dating had him at his wits' end. Between business travel, weekend travel to see Sharon, and weeknight evenings tied up in long phone conversations, Mark's life and responsibilities had become unmanageable. His bills went unpaid for weeks at a time, his laundry and dishes seemed to be piling up around him, and he never had time to call his parents or friends, or even just time to sit and reflect on his life. He'd lost the balance so necessary to a sense of contentment and peace. He was frazzled.

Sharon understood Mark's frustration. She says although the distance was a challenge for her, she always knew it was even more difficult for him. Since Mark was the one who did most of the commuting in their relationship, the stress of travel and of managing a home while on the road was all on his shoulders. When Mark told Sharon he thought they should break off the relationship, she wasn't willing to throw in the towel. She convinced him to think things through more carefully and see if they couldn't find a better solution to the problems they were having in the relationship. The couple already had plans to attend a friend's wedding, and Sharon told Mark she still wanted him to come. She figured that he wouldn't want to break up with her once they'd spent some time together and could talk face-to-face. "I told him I thought he owed it to me and the relationship to speak to me about it in person," she says.

As it turned out, Sharon was right. Breaking up over the phone had been easier on Mark because he was able to end the relationship without having to address his very real feelings for her. He says now, "The moment I saw her at the airport waiting for me, I realized I could never leave this woman." Instead, the two worked on a plan to ease the stresses of their long-distance relationship.

As they talked about Mark's concerns, the couple realized that between visiting Sharon, attending work conferences, and going to friends' weddings out of town, Mark had actually spent thirteen of the previous fifteen weekends away from home. He didn't even have time to catch his breath, let alone catch up on sleep, housework, or laundry. It was no wonder he felt stressed out.

Because Mark's happiness was important to her, Sharon suggested the couple spend an entire six weeks apart, staying at their respective homes. For a couple used to seeing one another three weekends out of every month, six weeks apart was going to require a real shift in how they thought about and managed their long-distance relationship. It was a difficult adjustment because they

Reality Check

Myth: The success of a long-distance relationship requires the couple to spend as much time as possible together over weekends as well as during vacations from work or school.

Reality: Time together is important, but so is maintaining a healthy sense of balance in life. Most of us just are not cut out to travel every weekend. Keeping up with personal responsibilities, family relationships and friendships, and hobbies and interests are all vitally important to a person's overall sense of happiness and satisfaction with life—two crucial elements for relationship success.

weren't used to being apart for that long at a time, but the break ultimately succeeded in helping them once again achieve balance and regain their sense of living independently.

Although they took a break from travel, Sharon and Mark didn't take a break from their relationship. They communicated frequently by phone on evenings and weekends. They even set up special "phone date nights" on Saturdays. (See chapter 5 for creative suggestions about how you might try this with your partner.) Every evening, Mark would call Sharon before turning in for the night, just to say good night. Those late-night calls were important in helping the couple ward off loneliness during the long stretch apart.

Their newfound commitment to each other infused Sharon and Mark's relationship with a renewed sense of hope and excitement. Rather than focusing on the problems of their relationship, they were learning to focus on solutions, working through challenges together. "We knew that no matter what happened, we were both committed to making it work. We had a no-quit attitude that really changed things between us for the better," says Sharon.

Mark says he's grateful Sharon understood his need for time alone while they were dating long-distance. "I think her willingness to let me have the time I needed actually made me even more excited for the time when we would be able to be together for good."

Mark and Sharon are now happily married with a small child, and they credit their experiences in long-distance dating with helping make their marriage stronger today, particularly during times when Mark has to travel for work. Their experiences dating long-distance have helped Sharon be more understanding and patient about Mark's business travel, because she's better able to focus on and appreciate all the time he is there with her and their baby.

Throughout this chapter, we'll look at various practical issues that affect long-distance couples, from committing to make time together in the beginning of the relationship, to strategies for alleviating travel-related stress, to effectively negotiating time spent online and on the phone. Hopefully, the examples we'll provide will help you and your partner create your own strategies for relationship success.

RELATIONSHIPS TAKE TIME

This statement may seem to some like a no-brainer, but relationships take time if they are going to work out—time together, time talking to one another, time thinking about each other, time doing thoughtful things for one another. This is no less true of long-distance relationships. Partners who live far apart still need to invest their time in the relationship. In fact, long-distance dating often requires partners to invest even more time than they would in a same-city relationship, because lengthy phone calls and intermittent travel are par for the course in intercity dating.

When we first spoke with Andrew, he was uncertain about the future of his relationship. An actor, he'd started dating his girlfriend, Rebecca, during the last three months of a touring production. When the tour ended, he moved back to New York and she relocated to Los Angeles. While he was attracted to Rebecca and enjoyed spending time with her, he wasn't sure he really wanted to pursue the relationship long-distance. Ultimately, he decided not to. She was disappointed, but we think Andrew made the right decision. Why? Because without both partners having a strong commitment to the demands of long-distance dating, this kind of relationship never works out. Andrew's heart just wasn't in it. This was no fault of his; it was simply a sign that the relationship didn't hold enough promise in his eyes for the effort to be worthwhile. And although Rebecca was disappointed, we think she was better off finding out the true extent of Andrew's feelings before investing any more of herself in their relationship.

Five Phone Rules You Should Never Forget

Different people have different ideas about the ideal frequency and duration of phone calls. If this is an issue in your relationship, you may want to set some phone rules that are agreeable to both of you. Type up your rules and leave them by the phone so that you're never tempted to break them. When you and your partner are establishing your list, you may want to consider these general phone rules we think every intercity couple should live by:

1. **Set a day and time to call in advance.** Some couples find it necessary to talk every day. Others use daily email to fill in the gaps between less-frequent phone sessions. Planning for the call in advance lets you look forward to the time you will talk, and also ensures you're not in the middle of something else when the call comes. Don't get us wrong. A surprise call just to say "I love you" is always nice, but for longer conversations, scheduling the time is generally best. You may even want to designate one specific day and time each week for lengthier phone calls, perhaps on the weekend when free time is in greater supply and both of you are relaxed and happy.

2. **Know your calling plan.** Call during hours that won't break the bank.

3. **Agree to a time to say good night.** This is particularly important when one person doesn't enjoy spending time on the phone, when there's a difference in time zones, when one partner is a night owl and the other isn't, or when the phone bills are a significant concern. Don't wait until the end of the appointed conversation time to bring up any serious topic (such as the future of the relationship, fears of infidelity, or anything that might start an argument). These topics are best discussed when both partners are prepared to talk about

them and have set aside sufficient time for a good discussion of
the issues.

4. **Put aside other activities.** Your partner deserves your undivided
attention. Chances are, he or she won't feel too valued if you've got
the call on speakerphone so you can run the vacuum cleaner, for
example. Playing video games, thumbing through magazines, and
clicking away at the computer are all no-no's for long-distance
phone conversations. Since face time is so limited in an intercity
relationship, phone time is your time to put the focus on your
partner.

5. **Never, ever, ever break up over the phone.** Long-distance dating
relationships can be stressful. It's all too easy to threaten to break
up over the phone, but often that isn't the decision you'd be likely
to make if you and your partner were having the same conversation
in person. Assuming you began this relationship because you saw
potential for a lasting future together, then isn't it worth at least one
last face-to-face meeting before deciding whether or not to cash in
your chips? Arrange to meet on neutral turf—perhaps a midway
meeting point—and discuss the matter carefully. It may be the right
time to end the relationship, or it may just be a critical turning point
in your dating—an opportunity to build a commitment and solidify
your mutual goals.

NEGOTIATING PHONE TIME VERSUS ALONE TIME

We first introduced you to Tim and Tina in chapter 2. When Tina took a new job in a distant city, the couple struggled with communication issues they'd not had to face before. To further complicate matters, Tina's new job required her to work very long, strange hours. Some weeks she'd put in eighty or ninety hours just trying to establish herself in her new position. As a result, it wasn't always easy for Tim to reach her by phone. He would text message her cell phone frequently, hoping she'd call him back. More often than not, Tina didn't have the time to return his calls when she was at work. "It wasn't that I didn't want to talk," she says now, "but I needed to be able to call at a time when I could really focus on him."

That was difficult for Tim to understand at first, but once he was able to hear what his girlfriend was saying and set aside his fears that she was rejecting him, he realized that her communication needs were as valid as his own. The couple eventually worked through this problem by setting up specific times for Tim to call when Tina would be available to talk.

Other couples have used similar techniques to negotiate communication time boundaries. For Rob and Julie, high school sweethearts who ended up at different universities, discovering the right formula for phone time was a tremendous challenge. Quiet, reserved Rob felt hurt by Julie's seemingly constant unavailability to talk. Julie, for her part, was busy getting involved in activities and making new friends. "She was just doing what anyone trying to adjust to life in a new place might do, but it still hurt," Rob says. This took some real getting used to on his part, since the couple had always been able to talk whenever they wanted to when they lived in the same town. Rob's feelings of loneliness and isolation at his new school were compounded by growing insecurities around his relationship with Julie.

The change in their situation had left him feeling possessive, jealous, and generally unhappy with what he saw as a dismal future.

Gradually, the two found a happy medium in regard to their phone time. They discovered they could limit their calls to between half an hour and an hour each day, and still keep both partners satisfied. In addition to phone calls, they sent each other several emails a day. It wasn't so much contact that Julie felt stifled, but it also wasn't so little that Rob felt slighted. It ended up being the perfect solution to meet both their needs. Eventually Rob was able to feel more connected to Julie, as though she weren't that far away after all.

USING A MUTUAL CALENDAR

For Sheri and Todd, establishing firm dates for visits was a strong motivator in continuing their long-distance relationship. Todd lived in Montana, and Sheri lived in Idaho, in towns approximately four hundred miles apart. About midway between them was the town of Missoula. Sometimes one of them would drive the full four hundred miles for a visit, and other times they met in Missoula. Todd, a good organizer, began keeping a calendar for their planned visits. He and Sheri would email the calendar back and forth until they were sure they established visiting dates that would meet both their needs. The calendar took into consideration not only planned weekend visits, but also scheduled time apart and special events in other cities, such as a friend's wedding. The schedule wasn't set in stone and it allowed some flexibility when needed, but having a calendar helped them visualize their goals and plan their time from visit to visit. "It was important just to know we had another weekend to look forward to," Todd says. "It really helped stave off those lonely nights." Todd would initiate the planning process by sending Sheri a chart like this:

October 5–6	Regular weekend	Todd visits Sheri
October 12–13	Todd has guys' camping trip with Paul and Rick	No visit scheduled
October 19–20	Randy and Cali's wedding in Saint Paul	Todd and Sheri meet at Saint Paul airport; spend weekend in Saint Paul
October 26–27	Gail and Nick's Halloween Party in Helena	Sheri visits Todd—don't forget your costume!
November 2–3	Regular weekend	No visit scheduled
November 9–10	Regular weekend	No visit scheduled
November 16–17	Sheri's birthday	Meet in Missoula for special weekend getaway
November 21–24	Thanksgiving weekend	Todd visits Sheri; celebrate Thanksgiving with Sheri's family
November 30	Sheri attends Kayla's baby shower	No visit scheduled

The couple scheduled their visits two or three months in advance, and doing so saved them a lot of heartache. Just knowing when they'd next see each other made the times they couldn't be together a lot easier to bear. The longest period they spent apart was eight weeks, a time Sheri says was lonely and difficult, but not impossible. "When I got depressed, Todd would remind me to look at the calendar. I saw our next visit looming ahead of us, and that got me through those two months of not seeing him."

This was a lesson they learned the hard way. Before Todd set up the calendar, they used to play it by ear when it came to planning. It seemed they inevitably ended up with some confusion or miscommunication that led to a fight. In a typical situation, Sheri would get lonely and be ready for a visit. If Todd told her he had plans with the guys, or that he had to go out of town on business, she would feel rejected and uncertain of his love for her. Another problem they had with visiting only spontaneously is that frequently one of them would receive an invitation to a wedding or company party and expect the other to be available to go, but it would turn out that he

Seven Ways to Make Travel Less Stressful

One thing couples who date long-distance must learn to do is to make travel second nature, since it seems one partner or the other must constantly be on the road. Here are our top seven suggestions for making travel more enjoyable and less stressful:

1. **Plan to arrive home at least sixteen hours before your next workday.** If you need to get up for work at eight Monday morning, then plan to be home no later than four Sunday afternoon. Why sixteen hours? The thinking behind the formula is that you'll use approximately eight hours for sleep and the other eight hours for winding down and getting yourself ready for the stresses of the week ahead. That also gives you plenty of time to deal with unexpected travel delays, such as road construction or a canceled flight.

2. **Try audio books.** If you're driving, this can be a particularly enjoyable way to pass the time and make you feel as though your hours in the car have been productive in some small way, particularly if the book you've chosen is a novel you've been meaning to read or perhaps a self-help title to help you tackle an issue at work or in your personal life. This strategy can help alleviate the sense of having no time for yourself when you have to travel a lot.

3. **Don't be afraid to take a personal day.** If you have an eight-hour drive ahead of you, it's probably easier to do if you leave at ten in the morning and arrive in time for dinner, rather than working a full day and driving all evening, which would put you at your destination after midnight. You and your partner will both enjoy your visit more if you're able to take it at a leisurely pace and enjoy dinner out when you first get to town.

4. **Take work with you.** If you're going to fly, taking something to work on can help make the time spent sitting in an airport or on a crowded flight seem like it's been put to better use, and that can help you fend off the sense of wasted time that can plague a relationship in which travel is a factor.

5. **Take up a plane-friendly hobby.** Do cross-stitch, read murder mysteries, work crossword puzzles—anything you find enjoyable that can be done on a plane will help you relax during the hours in the air.

6. **Start an audio journal.** If you drive long distances, a small investment in a hands-free tape recorder can be worthwhile. It will allow you to record your thoughts as you drive. Again, the general idea is to learn to make the time you're on the road more productive.

7. **Write a letter to your Great Aunt Phyllis.** If you're traveling by plane, now is the perfect opportunity to finally write all those letters, thank-you notes, and holiday cards you've been meaning to get to. Take them along in your carry-on luggage. Completing a task that's been lingering on your to-do list will help you make good use of your travel time, and that may save you from feeling as though you're falling behind in your day-to-day life.

or she had traveled three of the last four weekends and wasn't willing to leave home again. That's why Sheri and Todd say that keeping a mutual calendar saved their relationship.

A simple plan, such as scheduling the next visit or deciding how to spend the holidays, can go a long way in building the bond between two people dating long-distance. A planning chart like the one used by Todd and Sheri facilitates conversation about frequency of visits, who's doing the driving, and how much time to spend with friends and family. These are important points to navigate in the course of a long-distance relationship. In fact, scheduling is one of the most vital aspects of goal setting in intercity dating, and is typically much more important than it is for a same-city couple.

When we were dating, we relied on our mutual calendar to help us manage the practical aspects of travel and time and make visits more tangible—a good motivator when the distance got hard to bear. A mutual calendar is a good way for you and your partner to get on the same page. By monitoring not only your planned get-togethers but also your separate activities, you'll be better prepared for the weeks ahead.

Tip: **Make sure in your planning that time alone with your partner is a top priority, or else your relationship will pay the price. Intercity couples quickly learn that time alone together is a treasured thing; don't sacrifice it just to squeeze something else into your schedule.**

A mutual calendar will also allow you to analyze how you're spending your time. For instance, if you look at your recent and planned activities and notice that your partner is doing all the traveling, you may want to try to rearrange your plans so the travel is a little more balanced. If you see that the next three visits you've scheduled involve spending time with friends and family, you might consider adjusting your schedule so there's more time for the two of you to be alone.

Tip: **If the distance between you makes for a long drive, then why not split it in half and meet somewhere in between? This is not only a great way to get together, it's also a fun minivacation that both of you can enjoy. Figure out what interesting places you'd like to visit that aren't too far for either of you. Whether it's a romantic bed-and-breakfast, a chic downtown hotel, or a rustic state park, you're guaranteed to find some fun places that you'll both be able to enjoy while reducing the distance you each need to travel.**

One simple way of keeping a mutual calendar is to create a shared account on a website like Yahoo! or MSN. These sites allow you and your partner each to access a shared calendar, creating appointments, setting reminders, and using other special features. This way, either person can add an event, and that event will be instantly viewable by both of you.

Another way to organize a mutual calendar is by using a spreadsheet. This method is similar to the chart used by Todd and Sheri, only in this case, the end result is a little more conducive to analyzing how you're spending your time. On the next page is an example of a spreadsheet created by another couple, Brian and Kelly. You can see how the couple's detailed notes help facilitate discussions on the balance of time spent traveling, time spent together, and time spent with others.

WEEKEND OF	KELLY TRAVELS	BRIAN TRAVELS	KELLY & BRIAN	KELLY, BRIAN, FRIENDS & FAMILY	DETAILS
August 03					No visit scheduled
August 10	X	X	X		Meet halfway
August 17		X		X	Camping with friends
August 24					No visit scheduled
August 31	X		X		Labor Day weekend at Brian's
September 07					No visit: Football game with friends
September 14		X	X		Weekend at Kelly's
September 21					No visit scheduled
September 28					No visit: Lisa's bridal shower
October 05		X		X	Kelly's mom's birthday
October 12		X		X	Lisa's wedding
October 19					No visit scheduled
October 26		X		X	Halloween at Kelly's

In this example, the Xs in the second and third columns indicate who will be doing the traveling each weekend. The Xs in the fourth and fifth columns represent how Brian and Kelly will be spending their time together: alone, with each other, or with friends and family.

By examining this calendar, Brian and Kelly will likely see some trouble on the horizon. Out of the thirteen weekends listed, Brian is traveling six times, whereas Kelly only travels twice. Some of their plans could be shifted around to bring a better balance to the travel requirements. Another potential hazard is that a lot of time in October has been designated to spend with friends and family, without a single weekend planned for time alone together.

Seeing your social life in this way helps put it into perspective, making it easier to change plans and prevent problems from developing. A spreadsheet like this one facilitates planning as well as communication.

Spending hours laboring over mutual calendars, negotiating phone time, and talking about the stresses of travel inherent in a long-distance relationship is certainly nobody's idea of fun. But it is some of the basic groundwork that must be accomplished if you want your intercity relationship to succeed. In the initial months of dating, this kind of planning and work may not seem necessary at all. That's because both partners are typically so swept up in the excitement of new love that the difficulties of travel and time management seem like only minor hassles, if they seem like problems at all. But if these logistics aren't worked out, over time they can lead couples to significant resentments and can ultimately destroy even sound relationships, relationships that may have thrived in a same-city situation. By planning ahead and negotiating about travel and time in the early phases of the relationship, both you and your partner will be spared lots of headaches—and arguments—down the road.

Chapter Seven

KEEPING IT REAL:

Making Your Time Together Genuine

Lori met Kevin at a ski resort in Vermont. She was vacationing from Michigan; he was a food critic living in town. Although she had her misgivings about starting a long-distance relationship, Kevin's interesting lifestyle and relaxed outlook appealed to her. The two began dating and managed to see each other once every three weeks. In the beginning, everything seemed wonderful. Lori says Kevin was the quintessential romantic, making every effort to be sure she was happy as he swept her off her feet.

After three months, the relationship changed. Lori says things just fizzled out. Throughout their brief relationship, she says she never really felt like she knew him. "The whole time we were dating, I kept wondering when I was going to see the real Kevin," she says. Unfortunately, she never felt as though she did.

When two people date in the same city, they have plenty of opportunities to spend time together in a variety of circumstances, doing a wide range of things. Same-city partners are able to spend time together on weekends and during the workweek. They spend private time together as well as social time with each other's family and friends. They spend time going out to movies and restaurants, but they also spend time together just watching TV or eating leftovers from the fridge. Over the course of just a few months, same-city partners can get a real glimpse into each other's day-to-day reality, from the excitement of special outings to the ordinariness of mundane life. The relationship paints a relatively complete picture, and within a few months, each partner should have a fair idea of whether or not it has future potential and is worth pursuing for the long term.

When two people date long-distance, their perspective shifts. Because they see each other so infrequently, they tend to focus on "making each moment count." More often than not, that translates to going on extra-special dates, canceling time with family and friends to focus on the relationship, paying extra-special attention to always looking their best, and making sure they're on their best behavior whenever they're together.

Making the most of limited time together is not a bad thing. In fact, that concept is essential to the survival of any long-distance relationship. But being on our best behavior also comes at a price— we do so at the expense of being our genuine selves. As Lori describes it, "With Kevin, I always felt the need to be 'on'—like I needed to keep up appearances and make sure he would want to come back. We never just spent time vegging out to movies in our sweats, stuff like that."

This sense that long-distance dating can tend to lack emotional authenticity is something many men experience as well. Jack, a short-order cook in West Virginia, describes his intercity relationship in similar terms. Like Lori, Jack says he felt the need to make a good impression on his long-distance partner. The pressure to be on his best behavior made it difficult to express his real feelings. Since he was only able to visit his long-distance girlfriend infrequently, he was afraid that any expression of discontent on his part could ruin the relationship. "We hardly ever saw each other, so I didn't want to ruin it. Every date felt like an audition," he says. "I knew if I blew it, it might be the last time I'd see her."

Teresa and her long-distance boyfriend, Sean, met through an online dating service. Teresa hadn't been particularly interested in pursuing a long-distance relationship when they met, but since Sean lived in the same town as her mother and stepfather, she decided to be open to the idea. She already came back to visit family every month or so, so a new relationship seemed like just one more reason to make the trip. At first, the situation was ideal. "There were never any awkward moments deciding who would sleep where, because at the end of our dates, he would drop me off at Mom's house and go back to his apartment," Teresa says.

There were other benefits, too. The couple built a strong emotional and intellectual bond almost from the start. Email communication made it easy to talk freely about ideas and feelings. Each found it easier to collect their thoughts in an email than it would have been had their conversations taken place face-to-face.

While this kind of emotional intimacy may sound ideal—and in many ways it is—there is a downside. Although online communication can bring intimate discussions to a deeper level, Sean and Teresa discovered a difficulty common to long-distance partners. They understood each other on so many levels. They knew each other's thoughts on religion and politics and had shared many long discussions on life goals, fears, and dreams. But, although they knew so many deeply personal things, they hadn't had the chance to learn the mundane details of one another's day-to-day life, the stuff most same-city couples learn in the early weeks of dating.

As Teresa describes it, "Our emotional bond felt so real, so passionate, and it was. But for as deeply as I felt I knew his inner soul, I don't think I knew much about what he was like in his regular, day-to-day life." This was a problem that required some adjustment when the two made the commitment to live in the same city. When they first moved in together, they thought every day would be a fantastic, romantic adventure. Neither of them ever expected to discover a very real, very boring side to life together.

So are all long-distance relationships doomed to an artificial sense of emotional closeness? We don't think so. But it takes sincere effort to keep the relationship real and to build a genuine, deep understanding of one another when your partner lives miles away. In fact, we think keeping it real is one of the greatest challenges facing long-distance couples. That's because the everyday familiarity that normally develops in same-city relationships does not naturally occur when partners live far apart. For some people, like Lori and Kevin, this challenge spells the end of a long-distance relationship. For others, like Teresa and Sean, it may not bring an end to the relationship, but it can cause unforeseen difficulties in maintaining closeness and mutual satisfaction down the road.

Ten Signs Your Relationship Is "Real"

Is your relationship the real deal, or are you caught up in a fantasy of perfect dates and a perfect partner? Go through our list and see how your romance stacks up:

1. You've seen your partner on at least one "bad hair day."

2. You and your partner occasionally disagree.

3. You can name at least one of your partner's pet peeves.

4. You've spent lazy time together on visits, watching TV or playing cards.

5. You can name at least three things about your partner that annoy you.

6. You would be comfortable if your partner saw you while you were sick.

7. You know details about your partner's daily life (work, family, and/or school).

8. You know your partner's feelings toward his or her family.

9. You've met your partner's family and closest friends.

10. You've spent at least one major holiday with your partner.

REMEMBERING THE LITTLE THINGS THAT MEAN A LOT

One of the most difficult aspects of long-distance dating can be that emotional support can be harder to give—and receive—when your partner is miles away. Such was the case for Ken, a police officer whose girlfriend, Lauren, moved out of town to attend art school full time. He remembers that the most difficult part of dating Lauren after she moved was that she wasn't always there when he felt he really needed her. On one particularly tough occasion, he had been having a lot of trouble dealing with changes at work, and he deeply wanted her there to listen and show she cared. Not only was she not there in person; he couldn't reach her by phone due to different work schedules and a difference in time zones. Today, Ken says he doesn't know exactly how they worked through it; they just did. "We just stuck together, and eventually the hard times passed." Of course, the same holds true of any relationship whether or not distance is a factor. Every relationship is destined to have problems at one time or another. As Ken says, "You hit rough spots, and you don't see how it's ever going to work out. But if it's meant to be, somehow everything turns out just fine."

Even the seemingly trivial, mundane activities of daily life can take on new significance when the person you love isn't there to share them with you. Elaine, an elementary school teacher whose boyfriend, Alan, recently moved to a new city for a promotion, found herself missing the little details of their same-city relationship, even trips to the grocery. What she discovered when Alan moved was that he had grown to be an integral part of her life. Being away from him suddenly felt like a tremendous loss; she missed the familiarity and comfort of all they had shared in their same-city relationship.

For Elaine and Alan, keeping the relationship real has meant seeing each other as frequently as possible. Their goal is to see each other twice a month. Although this isn't always possible, they try not to let the time between visits extend too long beyond that goal. Frequent visits, including time set aside for going out with other couples and attending social events together, have helped them stay connected and feel like a "regular" couple. By incorporating each other's friends, families, and daily routines into their relationship, they've been able to maintain a sense of normalcy in their relationship in spite of the miles between them.

One of the often-overlooked elements essential to long-distance dating success is empathy. Empathy goes beyond sympathy, allowing us to really imagine life in our partner's shoes and opening us up to having more interest in those daily details of one another's lives. It's easy to be involved in the little things in a person's life when we see that person every day, but long-distance, keeping a sense of normalcy takes work. Empathy helps make it easier to focus on our partner's day-to-day life experience, and that is vital to long-distance dating success.

Tip: **Don't avoid arguments, but always argue fairly. Just because you're dating long-distance, you shouldn't feel afraid of occasional conflict. Healthy arguments can be good for a relationship and can help you learn to understand and respect one another's views while at the same time teaching you important skills for conflict resolution. But never argue in a personal, aggressive, or attacking manner. It's always better to remind yourself to listen carefully to your partner's point of view and make it your objective to understand his or her view as well as to help him or her understand yours.**

UNTANGLING THE MYTH OF QUALITY TIME

When you're dating long-distance, time is a precious commodity. Arguments often revolve around time—time spent together, time spent with friends, time spent alone, time spent on the phone, time spent arguing about how time should be spent. The issues are seemingly endless. No matter what your particular long-distance dating situation, the one thing there is never enough of is time.

Somewhere along the line, it seems, people arrived at the idea that "quality time" could replace "quantity time." Even if we couldn't spend our daily lives in one another's company, we were told, as long as the time we did spend together was focused and concentrated, the relationship would receive the nourishment it needed to survive. Not so! Time is to a relationship what water is to a growing plant. It is sustenance. Without sufficient time focused on the relationship, it will wilt.

So what does that mean for long-distance couples? The time you get to spend in the same place can be extremely precious, and the way you spend that time *is* extremely important. However, "quality time" doesn't necessarily equate to doing anything special—some of the best quality time for couples is just spent in each other's company, looking into one another's eyes and talking about the things that matter most. And in long-distance dating, as in any dating relationship, the amount of time together is as important, if not more important, than the purposeful "quality" of that time. That's because a genuine, loving relationship with lasting potential will reveal itself in the ordinary moments of daily living.

Real relationships aren't built over expensive dinners out as much as they are built cooking together in the kitchen. They aren't built sitting next to each other in silence at concerts and plays as much as they are built playing board games, taking a walk, or relaxing together in front of a warm fireplace. Sure, it can be fun to go to exciting places or try new things, but when you're dating long-distance, it's important that you use time together to create the emotional closeness that only comes from knowing another person's ordinary life. In other words, it's important not to make time together so "special" that you lose sight of what's inherently special in a normal, everyday relationship.

When we were dating long-distance, we used to make a point of doing ordinary activities together as much as possible. For example, even though we knew we'd only have forty-eight hours together, we'd usually spend some of that time doing the grocery shopping for the weekend. We didn't consider it time wasted. Instead, we looked at it as precious time learning more about each other's likes and dislikes. (Where else, for instance, would we have learned about our mutual love for anchovy paste, or that we both liked to eat yogurt with lunch every day?) Some of our favorite memories of those times are from the most ordinary of activities—walking Kate's dog, playing card games on the floor, heading to the Laundromat with a pocketful of quarters, cooking up dinner on the hibachi. And now that we're married, they are some of the same activities we do together today.

GOING FROM LOCAL TO LONG-DISTANCE

When a relationship that has been local must suddenly make the transition to long-distance, more effort is generally required of both partners to keep the relationship afloat. This was the case for Debbie and Chad. They met during Debbie's freshman year of college and from that moment on were hardly ever apart. When Chad graduated, he found himself stationed at an Air Force base in Arizona, while Debbie finished up her final year of school in Ohio. Since the couple had been dating locally for the past four years, being apart required

Eight "Real" Activities to Share with Your Partner

The next time you and your partner spend time in the same place, try some of these "real" activities to bring your relationship down to earth:

1. **Spend Sunday morning reading the paper together.** Knowing which section your partner reaches for first can give you a world of insight.

2. **Have a "sweat suits only" day.** Hole up in front of a few DVDs and just relax.

3. **Order a pizza.** Fancy restaurants are okay from time to time, but sometimes it's more fun to just hang out at home.

4. **Take a drive in the country.** Sometimes a little fresh air and some time where life is simple is just what the doctor ordered—the relationship doctor, that is.

5. **Take a walk.** A relaxed, leisurely walk through the neighborhood provides a great opportunity to talk and really connect.

6. **Make dinner together.** A trip to the grocery store and an hour or two in the kitchen can be more romantic than an evening on the town.

7. **Spend time with the family.** Getting to know the other people who are important to your partner is a great way to learn more about the person you're with.

8. **Go window-shopping.** A slow, leisurely walk along small-town streets invites lots of hand holding.

a significant change in their relationship. The distance between the two cities was a challenge from the start, particularly for a young couple without the financial resources for frequent travel. And the trip was a long one—two and a half days by car or four hours by plane.

The couple had known that a long-distance relationship was always in their future; when Chad graduated he'd be commissioned as an air force officer, which meant he'd end up stationed in another state—possibly as far away as Alaska. And although they knew that distance was an inevitability, they weren't fully prepared for the difficult adjustment.

The couple shared mutual goals and had discussed marriage before Chad moved to Tucson. Debbie, who wasn't yet ready to take that step, told him she thought they should take one day at a time and see what happened. Her goal was to finish school, and she didn't want to be engaged while she was a student, since her primary objective at that point was to focus on graduating. The couple had talked about Debbie moving to Tucson after she graduated, but their plans weren't yet certain. Like many young people, they knew they loved each other, but they just weren't ready to rush into marriage. That's how they began seeing each other long-distance.

Neither Chad nor Debbie had ever been involved in a long-distance relationship, so the challenges presented were new and often surprising. Like so many couples making the transition to long-distance dating, their greatest challenge was in learning to cope with the physical distance, especially when one or the other was going through a difficult time and just wanted a hug or a shoulder to cry on.

For couples who can't easily make the trip to see one another, keeping a sense of authenticity in the relationship when physical contact is infrequent can present a unique challenge. One easy way Debbie found to keep their relationship feeling real was to talk about Chad frequently to family and friends. Bringing him into her conversations helped support a sense that he was an active presence in her life.

Both partners were equally committed to making the long-distance situation work. "Making the effort to make it work meant everything to me, because I loved her," Chad explains. "I wanted her to be with me as soon as she graduated."

When Debbie finished school the following year, she moved out to Arizona to be with him, and the couple was married the year after that. Today, they're back in Ohio raising their first child. Even though it was challenging, they don't regret the year they spent apart. They say the best part of dating long-distance, for them, was that the time apart made them more appreciative of one another. Although the distance tested their love for each other in many ways, the end result was a profound sense of certainty regarding their future together. As Chad discovered, "If a relationship is meant to be, a couple will do everything in their power to make it last forever."

TURNING TIME APART INTO TIME TOGETHER

In chapter 5, we discussed the importance of creativity in long-distance dating. With a little sense of fun and a healthy dose of imagination, even time apart can feel like time spent together. The trick is to carefully orchestrate your efforts to make the relationship feel as close as it can, even if your partner is half a world away. This was something Carrie and Bob discovered through trial and error in their intercontinental relationship.

When they first met, both were students in the same graduate program. They were acquaintances in the same social circle, but Bob was married at the time. Their relationship was friendly, but nothing more. Bob's then-wife lived in a city five hours' drive from his graduate school, so she and Bob carried on a long-distance marriage for six months. That marriage ended in divorce after Bob discovered that his wife had been unfaithful to him while they were living apart.

Tip: **Being lonely in your long-distance relationship is one of the surest paths to resentment, and that can be extremely damaging to a dating relationship. Spend time cultivating your own interests and friendships. You'll probably have a more well-rounded life as a result, and you won't have to feel deprived of human connection. Plus, you'll have lots of interesting experiences to share with your partner.**

After his marriage ended, Bob began to see Carrie in a new light. He was attracted most to her warmth and compassion, and her friendship. She helped him through a very rough time in his life, and he says that's when he knew he loved her. The two began seeing each other, and a romantic relationship started. Eventually, they moved in together. After four years of dating, the relationship led to a proposal and, shortly after that, a long-distance engagement.

Both were earning Ph.D.'s in sociology when Bob, who was working on his dissertation at the time, was offered a research position at a university in England. The post was to last two years. The opportunity was too good to turn down. Carrie, who still had another three years of school ahead of her, decided to continue with her studies at the American university where she and Bob met. With an end date in mind, the couple decided they would continue their relationship long-distance, postponing wedding plans until they could once again be in the same city.

Communication Starters

Open up a dialogue with your partner and start working out the best strategies to keep your own relationship feeling real. The following questions can provide a starting point for discussion, but don't limit your conversation to the topics here. Remember, whatever matters most to each of you individually is what will be most important to maintaining a sense of normalcy in your own unique relationship:

- What does it mean to have normalcy in a relationship?

- What aspect of distance is currently the biggest obstacle in keeping a sense of normalcy in your relationship?

- What parts of your relationship feel real? What parts seem less so? Why?

- What can you each do to help your relationship feel more normal, in spite of the distance?

- Do you spend your time together in the best way possible? Could you better use your time to help the relationship feel more genuine?

Even though the new situation forced the couple to spend most of their time apart, they soon discovered that creative communication strategies could help them feel more connected in spite of the physical distance between them. As we've already discussed, good communication is critical to long-distance relationship success. But frequency of communication is as important as the quality of communication. It's not enough just to talk about the big issues. You have to make time to talk about the little day-to-day details of life too, since it's part of having a healthy, genuine relationship. For Carrie and Bob, frequent contact has been a must. The couple emails each other first thing every morning and before going to bed each night. They chat online once a day and plan "phone dates" a few times a week. They also send letters and photos and make the occasional surprise phone call, too.

Perhaps the biggest challenge for this couple has been keeping a sense of normalcy in their relationship. The adjustment from being with one another every day, going to sleep in the same bed, and waking up next to each other, to suddenly having very limited physical contact has required a huge adjustment. The challenges have been compounded by the incredible distance, both in actual miles and in time—a five-hour time difference. Bob is just going to bed when Carrie gets home from school, and when she wakes up in the morning, he's already having lunch.

Carrie says that keeping the relationship genuine is a constant effort. She finds the limits to their talk time very frustrating and the challenges of the time difference particularly daunting. "Often I think of things I want to tell him," she says, "but I can't just call, so I might forget about it."

The one thing that has remained constant is the couple's love and commitment to each other. "If the love is strong and the commitment base is tight, then people in long-distance relationships can make it work," Bob says. "A relationship will hold up regardless of whether the people live in the same household. If a relationship ends during or after living long-distance, then it would have ended anyway." We tend to agree.

FINDING NORMALCY WHEN RELATIONSHIPS START OUT LONG-DISTANCE

How do you create normalcy in a relationship that begins long-distance? This can certainly be even more of a trick than it is for couples that start their dating relationship in the same city. That's because, for couples beginning with the disadvantage of distance, exactly what *is* normal to their relationship is still a mystery. Think about it. If you've only ever seen your partner on Saturdays and Sundays, how would you know what he or she is like during the workweek? If you only visit your partner during scheduled trips, how would you know what your partner's typical day looks like? Well, for starters, you ask.

Although we've said it many times before, this single point cannot be overstressed: Nothing is more critical to the success of a long-distance relationship than communication. When you date long-distance, you have the benefit of written communication on your side, which is often an even more powerful tool even than face-to-face conversations, particularly during the early phases of a relationship when you're just getting to know the other person.

"Email is the modern-day love letter," says Danielle, a woman who met her husband online and dated long-distance for just over a year before tying the knot. "In an email message, you can pour out your emotions and really get to know the other person." (See chapter 2 for ideas on successful email communication.)

When we first began dating, this was true for us. Remember that Tom Hanks–Meg Ryan movie *You've Got Mail*? Both protagonists were so excited each time they booted up their computer, anxious to see if they had a new message waiting from their online love interest. That's how we felt every time we opened our inboxes. It was a great feeling. We got to know each other through those messages, and even today, we look forward to starting out our workday with the hopes of seeing a little love note in our daily email. It's part of the fabric of our ongoing love story.

LOVE IN A PRESSURE COOKER

Even with all the love in the world, long-distance dating presents challenges to establishing and maintaining a comfortable sense of normalcy in day-to-day living. Often the most pressure comes during time spent together. Bob says that has definitely been the case in his and Carrie's relationship. "You want to try to reestablish that physical and emotional link in a relatively short time period," he explains. "Plus, you just want to catch up on what's happened in each other's day-to-day life."

Carrie agrees. Since she and Bob rarely see each other (and when they do, it's usually for no more than ten days), the couple generally tries to do a lot of things when they're together. If he visits her, they try to do all the things they used to do when they shared an apartment. They go to their favorite restaurants or go to the movies and seldom spend time with others, believing that they always need to maximize their time together. This sense of having to cram a lot of dating into a short visit was a common complaint among the couples we interviewed. Sometimes just maintaining a long-distance relationship can be exhausting work.

Dawn, a restaurant hostess, told us that her visits with her long-distance boyfriend, a musician named Patrick, are typically such whirlwind experiences that they leave her feeling exhausted every time they're over. The couple's flexible work hours allow for visits that last three or four days at a time. "During those few days," she says, "I'm on my feet more than I am when I'm working—all we do is run, run, run."

The Four Must-Haves of International Dating

Here are a few things we think every international couple must have for dating success:

1. **Affordable long-distance rates.** In many countries, you can buy discount international phone cards. In western Europe, for instance, it is possible to purchase two to three hours of phone time to the United States for just a few euros. Not sure where to find them? Check out the currency exchange booths in train stations and airports.

2. **An extra clock.** Keep a clock set to your partner's time zone. This will help you remember the best times to call. It will also help you feel connected to your partner.

3. **Email.** Even if one of you doesn't have a computer, try to find out where you can access the Internet (libraries, coffee shops, etc.) and try to keep emails as regular as possible.

4. **A camera.** Be sure to share photographs frequently, either through email or in letters. Pictures provide a vivid glimpse into each other's daily life, which is essential when cultures and experiences are so different.

Dawn says that by the time she's ready to pack her bags and come home, she typically feels so irritable that their final hours together are stressful and upsetting. The couple has discussed possible solutions to this problem and have come to the conclusion that the success of their relationship is going to depend on taking a much more relaxed approach.

Patrick says it's hard to relax knowing that his time with Dawn is so limited. Each visit he finds himself thinking that, since it's probably going to be a while before he sees her again, he needs to make the most of every minute. The couple goes to restaurants, movies, malls, sporting events, amusement parks, and museums—all over the course of a few short days. "In a way," he says, "it's fun because we're doing all the things I always think I want to do but never seem to make the time for. But in another way, it's really frustrating, because we're always going at such a fast pace."

That experience can be even worse if your time together is limited to two days every other weekend, or every other month, as it is for many couples. Most intercity relationships allow for only weekend visits, and that can seem particularly stressful to couples trying to work a month's worth of dating into just forty-eight hours.

Our best advice? Just have fun. Sure, you can plan special dates, but don't allow yourselves to lose sight of the real reason you're spending time together. You don't need to make each visit a momentous occasion. That kind of pressure isn't healthy for any relationship, especially a long-distance relationship, which already comes with its own share of unique pressures and stresses. It's much more important to make each visit an opportunity to see new aspects of your partner and to build the foundation of emotional connection and strong communication that will see you through weeks of not seeing one another in person. If you learn that, your relationship will have a much better chance at long-term success.

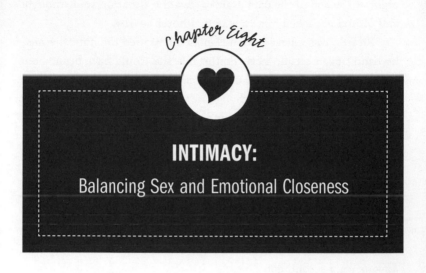

Chapter Eight

INTIMACY:
Balancing Sex and Emotional Closeness

"When I first met Ricardo, there was an instant spark," says Danika, a data processor in Montana. "I think I knew from the start he was the man I would marry."

He called her after the two met on a three-day cruise each had taken with friends. He asked her out on their first date three weeks later and offered to fly out to Montana from Illinois. She didn't want Ricardo to think she didn't like him, but at the same time, she wanted to make sure it would be easy enough to say good night at the end of the date. Danika gave the situation some thought and ultimately asked him to stay in a hotel nearby.

Ricardo was relieved when Danika mentioned the hotel, because he hadn't been certain how comfortable she would have been about him staying over. He knew she was special, and he didn't want to rush things. He says that although he was extremely attracted to her and wouldn't have objected if she'd asked him to spend the night, he also didn't want to risk ruining things by moving too quickly.

For Danika, the hard part came the second time he made a visit. The couple had been communicating by phone and email every day for two months. "After getting to know him that well over email, I was already madly in love with him—of course I wanted him to stay the night. But I had to remind myself it was only our second date, and I wouldn't have been comfortable with the decision to sleep with anyone on a second date."

Ideally, as a relationship develops emotionally, a couple is able to initiate and pursue physical intimacy at whatever pace and with whatever limitations are comfortable for both people. This can be tricky when you only see each other once a month, especially when a relationship is just starting out.

In this chapter, we'll discuss the issues of sex and intimacy that affect new intercity relationships, including initiating conversations about expectations and desires, introducing sexuality, and postponing sexual involvement until both partners feel the time is right. Because some relationships already have a sexual element prior to becoming long-distance, we'll also address how distance can change a preexisting sexual relationship, with real-life strategies for coping with the physical and emotional isolation that comes when your partner is far away. Finally, we'll discuss the importance of maintaining a balance between sexuality and other aspects of your relationship when you are together and give practical strategies for making that balance a priority.

COPING WITH THE PRESSURE TO BE SEXUALLY ACTIVE

Carolyn and Matthew met in college when she was a senior and he was a sophomore. They first met at the surprise birthday party of a mutual friend, although Carolyn, who wrote for the school paper, had actually reviewed Matthew, an actor, in a campus production eight months previously. "Fortunately, I gave him a good review!" she laughs now.

The two connected on a number of levels. She liked his smile and that he could make her laugh. Also, Matthew had mentioned his high level of involvement in his Christian church. Carolyn, who was herself seeking a religious affiliation, wanted to learn more not only about Matthew but about his religion as well.

Three months after they started dating, she graduated and moved to New York City to pursue a career in publishing, while he stayed on as an acting student in Connecticut. The distance between their two cities was about seventy miles—close enough to make frequent visits possible, but far enough to make an ongoing relationship somewhat challenging. After he graduated, Matthew moved to a town in New York state that was closer to Carolyn, but still an hour away. The couple dated exclusively long-distance before making a permanent home in New York City when they tied the knot, three and a half years later.

In spite of the fact that both Carolyn and Matthew had been in other long-distance dating relationships that hadn't worked out, the decision to continue dating after Carolyn's graduation was an easy one. As with so many same-city couples who make the transition to long-distance dating, they felt that what they had was really special, and they wanted to stay together. Another factor that made long-distance dating appealing? At the time they started dating, both Carolyn and Matthew knew that their career goals would ultimately take them to New York, so they knew that distance would only be a factor in their relationship for a limited time, and this helped make the goal of being together someday much easier to imagine.

Even though their relationship wasn't as long-distance as many of the couples we spoke with, the miles between them were an issue in creating a sense of sexual pressure that was difficult to overcome. That's because the pressure-cooker effect discussed in the last chapter can apply to issues around physical intimacy as well. The less often you see your partner, the stronger the urge to make a connection. This created some conflict for Carolyn and Matthew. Both held a strong conviction that sexual intimacy should be saved for marriage. They felt that a healthy dating relationship shouldn't be focused primarily on sex and viewed dating as a chance to get to know the other person and to deepen their relationship slowly and carefully. Although they agreed sexual chemistry was an important element in their dating life, they also believed sexual intimacy would be damaging to their developing emotional relationship.

Not everyone shares this view, of course, but for those who do, long-distance dating poses a real challenge. As Carolyn explains it, "When you've been apart for a long time and then you see each other, there's a real temptation to be physically intimate because you're so overwhelmed by the other person's physical presence, maybe more so than you'd be if you saw them every few days." She says this created some difficulties in her long-distance relationship with Matthew. "We probably had a stronger sexual desire for each other because we were apart and then together, apart and then together."

The couple says the pressure to be sexually intimate was at times overwhelming. Still, they believe that, in spite of this pressure, there was a positive side to long-distance dating. The time apart allowed them to communicate verbally and through email, which might not have happened as much had they lived near one another. The distance forced the couple to get to know each other without getting lost in the euphoria and sexual attraction of a new relationship.

Now that they're married, they say the intimacy in their marriage is enhanced by the years they spent dating long-distance. The couple communicates well, thanks in part to learning to work things out verbally over the phone. They say they are not as likely to fall back on the physical aspects of marriage to fix their problems, as they suspect some couples might be prone to do.

Five Reasons Not to Rush Intimacy in a Long-Distance Relationship

Long-distance dating comes with more than its fair share of relationship pressures, including the pressure to be sexually intimate. Here are some reasons we think it makes sense to take it slowly. These guidelines certainly apply to young couples in high school or college, but even the most worldly couples can benefit when their relationships develop gradually:

1. **Meaning.** Sexual connection should have meaning in a relationship. Without a deep, shared commitment to the relationship and to one another, sexual expression is little more than a bodily function. You owe it to yourself to give your relationship time to develop.

2. **Relating.** Some couples think that sex will help bring them emotionally closer to their long-distance partner, but the truth is, using sex as a tool to create instant intimacy never works. It's far more likely that tactic will backfire, and the sparks will fizzle out long before a real connection is made.

3. **Mystery.** A little mystery is good for intercity romance. Holding onto that special aspect of yourself to give when the time is right only makes your partner interested in learning more about you as the relationship unfolds.

4. **Enjoyment.** Intimacy is just better when it is explored slowly, gradually. Take it easy and enjoy every step along your journey to real intimacy.

5. **Trust.** As we've discussed in previous chapters, trust and fidelity are essential to long-distance dating success. Never jump into a sexual relationship with someone you don't know well enough to say with complete certainty you can trust. It's not unromantic to have a little healthy skepticism at the beginning of a long-distance relationship—it's just good sense.

SETTING THE RIGHT PACE

As we've already seen, long-distance dating can create pressures to move a relationship forward sexually at a faster pace than might be comfortable for both partners. As JoEllen, a college student who met her boyfriend Mark on spring break, tells us, "Every time I see him, I feel like I need to give in sexually because I'm afraid he won't want to keep coming back if I don't." She's quick to point out that Mark isn't placing that pressure on her—it's something she's put on herself. Certainly there is a popular stereotype that men are only interested in sex. "There's so much sacrifice in a long-distance relationship," says JoEllen. "I guess I just figure there needs to be a payoff in order to make it worth the effort."

No one should ever have to feel as though they need to provide sexual gratification as a payoff for the investment required by a long-distance relationship. Think about it: If you're afraid your partner is dating you just for sex, wouldn't he or she do better to find that sort of relationship locally rather than enduring all the hassle of long-distance dating? The fact is, most people who date long-distance do so because they are deeply, genuinely interested in the other person—enough so to make all the effort and the loneliness and longing worthwhile.

Tip: **For couples in high school or college, the pressure to rush sexual intimacy can come from many powerful forces—friends, insecurity about whether partners really care for one another, and, of course, hormones. Just remember, none of these are good reasons to decide whether or not you're ready for this relationship-changing (and sometimes life-changing) step.**

So what is the right pace for developing intimacy in a long-distance relationship? We can't find that answer for you; it's something you'll have to work out on your own. But one thing is certain: if either you or your partner is uncomfortable or unsure if you're moving things along too quickly, then you're not going at the right pace for you. Sexual intimacy should be a meaningful and enjoyable experience for both of you, and it should never feel uncomfortable or pressured. If it does, that's a good sign that you should back off and allow things to cool down before going any further.

NOW THAT YOU'RE ON YOUR OWN

Coping with loneliness and isolation in a relationship that's transitioned from local to long-distance can be a real challenge. You may have been used to a certain level of sexual connection, and putting distance into the mix certainly changes that. It can create many difficult feelings associated with separation, including loneliness and a sense of sexual deprivation. Intimacy is tough when there are hundreds of miles between partners. Creativity is a must.

For some, being creative may involve phone sex or cybersex. Charlene, who uses her computer as a surrogate for sexual expression with her partner, says she never thought of herself as someone who would have cybersex. In fact, she says, "I always thought those people were such losers. But here I am, dating long-distance and using cybersex as a way to feel a little less lonely." Still, most of the couples we spoke to who had tried phone sex or cybersex confirmed our suspicions that both are poor substitutes for physical closeness.

If phone sex or cybersex is something you want to try but you feel too awkward to give it a go, take it slowly at first. Some couples told us they found flirting on the phone a fun way to keep their relationship romantic, making some suggestive comments here or there but never going so far as to experiment with phone sex. You might try describing what you're wearing if it's provocative (or make something up if it's not). You could also begin by describing a sexual dream or fantasy. One woman told us she used to talk to her boyfriend while she was taking a bath because she knew the sound of the water would get his imagination going. Other couples let their emails gradually become more and more erotic until they're comfortable with cybersex as a vehicle for sexual expression. Whatever you try, we suggest you keep a sense of humor about it, and don't be afraid to recognize when it's just not working. There's no need to force an erotic phone call or online chat if it isn't enjoyable for both of you.

Even if phone sex and cybersex aren't for you, most couples say the experience does help build a sense of closeness. Certainly there is real vulnerability involved in opening yourself up to something like that. Mariko and Curt's three-year relationship went long-distance when Curt took a job overseas. They found that phone sex and cybersex enhanced their intimacy and helped make the time between visits more bearable. Although these methods were a bit awkward the first time or two they tried, they say that eventually their creativity and willingness to try brought them closer together. Nevertheless, they'll be the first to admit that phone sex and cybersex are no substitute for the real thing.

Tip: **Disable the call waiting! Most phone setups have a code that allows you to disable call waiting before making a call. Nothing is worse than getting all hot and heavy only to be interrupted by your mother on the other line.**

If you've been in a relationship that has been sexually intimate and suddenly you find yourselves dating long-distance, you may be wondering if it's even possible to maintain a real relationship with so little physical contact. We say it is.

Ana, a woman whose boyfriend, Steve, accepted a one-year position in another town, says sexual intimacy is much less important in long-distance relationships than it is for those couples dating in the same city. She says that when her relationship with Steve became long-distance, their intimacy became more emotional and intellectual than sexual. In her view, not having the closeness of sex prompted them to find other ways to connect. This shift was actually healthy for their relationship, which had come to a point where they were uncertain of its future.

In fact, the distance gave them an opportunity to see one another on many different levels, not just sexually. Rather than creating demands, it actually removed the pressures of a sexual relationship, allowing them to focus on other aspects of their life together. That's when they realized that they wanted to be in the same place on a full-time basis. In fact, the couple was engaged just two months after Steve moved away.

Tip: **Avoid the webcam temptation. Some couples try using their webcams to send erotic emails. If you've considered it, we have two words for you: Paris Hilton. Sure, you and your partner get along great now, but what happens if you break up? Or perhaps worse, what happens if his little brother or her merciless roommate gets ahold of those files? Unless you want to run the risk of having your intimate moments splattered all over cyberspace, we suggest you find other ways to make an intimate connection.**

Still, there were downsides to having to put their sexual relationship on the back burner. "If we had a less-than-stellar weekend together and were fighting, there was huge pressure to kiss and make up before someone left to go back home," Ana tells us. "The worst was getting mad and not making that connection, and then regretting it a week later when we really needed it but were far apart."

A DELICATE BALANCE

As it turns out, finding the right balance between time alone in the bedroom and time doing other relationship-building activities is something nearly all long-distance couples struggle with. As one man we spoke with put it, "You get to see each other so infrequently, when you do get together, it's almost impossible not to act like a couple of lovesick rabbits." Other people we talked to jokingly used terminology like "sex-a-thon" and "conjugal visits" to describe their times together. Certainly, there is a fine line between forging intimacy during visits and focusing solely on sex.

For many couples, sexual involvement is an important part of staying connected to one another. This has been the case for Mariko and Curt. They say sexual intimacy is an important bonding factor for them as a couple. The fact that they had dated for so long before Curt moved helped them stay open when it came to discussing issues of intimacy. Because they were already very comfortable talking about a wide range of topics, communicating about intimacy has never posed any real problems.

What *has* been a problem is finding the right balance in how they spend their limited time together. First, there's the issue of the time difference. Because they live several time zones apart, jet lag has often had a negative impact on their intimacy. Often one partner is half-asleep while the other is wide awake. So timing their sexual intimacy on visits has become very important.

Second, there's the sense of sexual deprivation that long-distance couples often experience. "Since we only see each other every couple of months, our first reaction when we get together is to have sex," says Mariko. "It's an important part of our relationship, but we have to make sure that sex isn't all we do, because there are other things that are equally important for keeping that emotional closeness."

The distance has created some unrealistic expectations about sex in their relationship. "In a way, I think we may put too much pressure on ourselves during visits, and at times we may be a bit unrealistic about it," Curt says. "If you only have a week together, and part of that week involves traveling or visiting family, how can you begin to cram a month's worth of sexual intimacy in? It's pretty impossible." Acknowledging this challenge is the first step in working through it, so the couple has made finding a sexual balance a priority in their relationship.

These days, they make sure that when they see each other it's not all about sex. Mariko says it's equally important to use their time together to talk, laugh, and just cuddle on the couch. "Those things are necessary to maintaining a sense of connection," she says.

One way to ensure you achieve the right balance is to plan ahead. Ideally, of course, sex should be spontaneous and fun, but adding a little structure to your visits together can help ensure that you nurture every aspect of your relationship, not just sexuality. It's equally important to make sure you schedule enough time alone together for romantic encounters to happen naturally and not feel rushed. Mariko and Curt always make sure they have some private time when they visit each other. Since Curt lives with five other people, it's not easy to have privacy. To combat this problem, the couple spends some weekends at a romantic bed-and-breakfast.

If you and your partner are sexually intimate, visits provide an opportunity to build that side of your lives together, a side that is typically in short supply in long-distance dating. This can make your connection feel more intimate. As one woman told us, "We appreciated each other so much more when we were together, and were much more emotionally connected. It made the sex more special."

Perhaps more important, however, is that long-distance dating provides a unique opportunity to spend time developing other kinds of intimacy. So many people we've spoken with agree that dating long-distance can make or break a relationship because couples must rely more on talking and getting to know each other than on physical chemistry. Long-distance dating opens the door to a potentially deep and meaningful connection.

CONNECTING BEYOND THE BEDROOM

When you get right down to it, long-distance dating requires more emotional intimacy than just about any other kind of dating relationship. That's because dating long-distance demands that couples rely less on the intimacy of physical expression and more on the intimacy built through talking, sharing, laughing, and planning together. When your ability to connect physically is so limited, emotional intimacy becomes essential. Bren, an entrepreneur whose boyfriend, Ryan, lives just over an hour away, says long-distance dating is "much more of an emotional roller coaster than a normal relationship." She says distance has made it much more difficult to know what Ryan is thinking or feeling because she can't see or touch him. "So many arguments could have been ended with a simple hug or a smile, but that doesn't translate well over the phone, especially if you're tired or stressed." Nonetheless, she says her long-distance relationship has taught her many things, including the importance of emotional intimacy; when this key element is missing, it can signal the end of any relationship, regardless of locale.

Couples can be emotionally intimate without being in the same place. And while creating intimacy in a long-distance dating relationship isn't necessarily harder than in a same-city relationship, it does require a different approach. Building genuine emotional intimacy in an intercity relationship requires approaching the relationship from different angles. It's a trial-and-error process in which couples must explore together to find ways that work for them. There's no right or wrong way to build emotional intimacy in your long-distance relationship; all that matters is that you do.

Curt and Mariko know this firsthand. They admit that emotional intimacy is more of a challenge now than it was when they were living together. Curt says the closeness they feel after chatting online or sharing a phone call is always bittersweet, an ongoing reminder of the sadness he's felt since moving away. Although it may seem unlikely, the couple has actually discovered that the miles between them have been a positive factor in helping them achieve real intimacy. Like so many long-distance couples, they've learned just how much they mean to one another and that life isn't the same when they're apart. And this, in turn, has strengthened the bond between them.

If you take only one thing away from reading this chapter, we hope it is this: Intimacy isn't forged just by being in the same place. Lots of people have sexually active same-city relationships that aren't really that close at all. The truth is, your long-distance relationship can be as intimate and caring as you want to make it. In fact, you just may discover that real intimacy goes beyond the bedroom, and that emotional closeness is a bond that exists beyond physical distance.

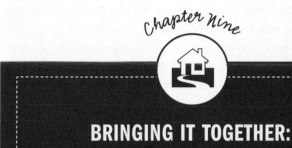

Chapter Nine

BRINGING IT TOGETHER:
When the Time Is Right to Live
in the Same Place

For most long-distance couples, the decision to take their relationship to a higher level ultimately involves one partner moving to the other's town. The long-anticipated day when an intercity couple can finally say good-bye to teary late-night phone calls, lonely Saturdays, and long commutes is truly a time of celebration. But making the transition from long-distance dating to dating locally presents its own unique challenges and potential pitfalls as well, and that can come as a surprise or even a disappointment to couples who aren't prepared for the change.

Cara says that when she moved to Boston to be with her boyfriend, Wes, she felt sure of her decision to move. He had a solid, established career in Boston, whereas she was just out of school and could start her career in any city she chose. In her mind, it was only logical that she should move. Even though she felt this way, the decision was still difficult. Before Cara graduated, the couple talked many times about marriage. Cara was confident that she and Wes wanted the same things from the relationship. "He certainly talked the talk," Cara says now. "He wanted me to move to Boston as badly as I wanted to be there." After graduation, she left her family and friends behind and moved in with Wes. Not long after that, she says she noticed a definite shift in his attitude toward long-term commitment.

The couple's discussions about marriage became less and less frequent, until finally they stopped altogether. Cara assumed Wes was saving for a ring, and decided not to spoil the surprise by bringing the subject up. After months passed with no proposal, she decided to ask him about it. Wes told her it would only be a matter of time. He said he did want to marry her, but that he'd hoped to give the relationship a full year of living together before taking that step. Cara was disappointed but tried to understand.

By the time she had lived with Wes for a year and a half, Cara was beginning to seriously doubt his commitment. Since she still hadn't received an engagement ring, she brought the subject up once more. Wes admitted that he wasn't really sure about the idea of marriage. He said he thought he might want to marry her someday but wasn't ready to commit. Cara was devastated. In her mind, she'd made that commitment a year and a half earlier, when she decided to uproot herself and move to Boston.

Take Our Commitment Quiz

Are you a true-blue companion or a commitmentphobe? Your answers to the following ten questions just may give you some surprising insights into your own commitment style:

1. Do you regularly take time out of your schedule to travel to see your partner, or do you let your partner do all the traveling?

2. Do you schedule time to talk to your partner on the phone on a regular basis (daily or every other day)?

3. Do you think about spending the future with your partner, beyond the few weeks ahead?

4. Do you and your partner seriously discuss the possibility of one or both of you relocating in the future?

5. Do you make plans for holidays and other special events with your partner's schedule in mind?

6. Have you introduced your partner to your parents and your close friends? If not, do you have plans to do so in the near future?

7. Do you talk about your partner and your relationship around coworkers (*including* the attractive ones)?

8. Have you lost any real romantic interest in other potential dating partners, or do you always feel the need to "keep one in the wings," in case your current relationship doesn't work out?

9. Would you be open to the possible compromise of moving one day, even if it isn't your ideal solution?

10. Can you imagine yourself married to your partner one day?

Different stages of dating require varying degrees of commitment for a relationship to flourish and grow. In this chapter, we'll talk about the commitment involved in going from long-distance dating to a same-city relationship. We'll also talk about common problems that can arise when a long-distance relationship suddenly becomes local. And we'll take a look at some of the signs that will help determine if you and your partner are ready for this life-changing step.

TALKING ABOUT THE "C" WORD

The decision to move for the sake of a relationship—to pick up your life, leave family and friends behind, and head to a new city—is a bold and daring act of love. It also requires great commitment. By the very act of moving, one partner is making a commitment to the other. That's why it's so important to make sure both partners have the same level of commitment before taking that life-changing step. And the place to begin that discussion is by talking openly about attitudes toward commitment.

Our attitudes toward commitment are influenced by a variety of factors. Whether our parents had a happy marriage, whether our friends are in committed relationships, and our own prior dating experiences all play a role in helping shape the way we look at commitment. Some people view commitment as a healthy sign of relationship growth; others see it as a "trap" designed to rob them of their independence. Whatever your view of commitment, one thing is nearly certain: if your partner's view is significantly different from yours, your relationship will eventually be headed toward disaster. When long-distance partners decide to make the move to a local relationship, sharing a mutual understanding of commitment is critical.

It's essential that both people discuss the serious level of commitment involved in one partner's decision to move. Broaching the

Communication Starters

Use the questions below to open up a dialogue about commitment with your partner:

- What does the word *commitment* mean to you? Do you view it as a positive or negative word?

- What commitments have you made in your life (commitments to a goal such as graduating or earning a promotion, commitment to a friendship or to family relationships, commitment to the care of a pet, financial commitments such as home ownership or school loans, and so forth)? Were these commitments easy or difficult, and why? What was the result?

- Do you believe that commitment is appropriate at different levels of a dating relationship? What would commitment look like at different stages of dating?

- Have you ever committed to a romantic relationship in the past? What was the result? How has that experience influenced the way you view commitment today?

- Do you believe that you're currently committed to your dating relationship? Why or why not?

- What, in your view, is the ultimate goal of your long-distance relationship?

subject of commitment can be difficult in any relationship. Many people (and, in spite of popular opinion, not only men) find that the word *commitment* can get them shaking in their boots. The easiest way to approach the issue may be to get the other person to bring it up first. Ask questions about your partner's thoughts and feelings on the relationship (the Communication Starters in this chapter are a good place to begin). If your partner doesn't take the cue, go ahead and bring the subject up directly, but don't do it when your partner is unlikely to be receptive to the conversation. Choose a time when you're both relaxed and happy. Finally, while we know it can be hard to get good face-to-face time in a long-distance relationship, we do recommend that you save this conversation for an in-person discussion. Some topics are best approached when you're together, and this is one.

If you and your partner decide you're ready to live in the same city but you're not ready for a lifetime commitment, then we think it's highly advisable to take up separate residences at first. We aren't just saying this because we want to make your grandma happy; it's good, plain sense. If you're moving to a new city to be with someone you're dating and there's no solid promise of lifetime commitment attached to that decision, you would be wise to find your own place. Living apart will help you build an identity in that city separate from the already-established home, friends, and activities of your partner. If the relationship doesn't work out, you may find yourself in a strange city with no job, no place to live, and no friends. Even though it may be unpleasant to think about, it's best to prepare for that possibility before it strikes.

Likewise, we suggest that if you're moving to another city with the intention of committing to marriage, you make sure that commitment is understood fully by both parties before packing your bags. It's the best way to protect you both and make sure you have the same goals. (For a refresher on establishing and communicating goals in a relationship, take another look at chapter 3.)

In our own long-distance dating situation, frequent conversations about marriage finally led to the decision to move our relationship to the next level. Chris left his job in South Carolina and we bought a house together in Ohio, with the express agreement that a formal engagement would be in our immediate future. So when Chris proposed a few weeks later, it may not have been as much of a romantic surprise as it is for some couples, but that was okay by us. We didn't need a surprise as much as we needed a solid plan for our future. It was this guarantee of trust and commitment that provided the foundation on which our long-distance relationship could finally become a lifelong, same-city marriage.

So, how long is too long to wait for someone to commit? Though the answer to this question varies from person to person, in general the answer can be found by asking yourself how long you're satisfied waiting. Remember, even if this person doesn't want to commit to you, there's someone out there who will. You owe it to yourself to take the time to find that person and live the happy life you deserve.

MAKING THE LEAP

"At first, I never even considered the concept of committing to my long-distance relationship with Jenn," says Charlie, a twenty-seven-year-old who eventually married his long-distance girlfriend. He says moving wasn't always on his list of priorities. Because the couple had successfully negotiated ways to make the distance less of a factor and were having such a good time together, thinking about the next step hadn't crossed his mind at all.

The subject was very much on Jenn's mind, however. After about nine months of long-distance dating, she brought up the topic of their future together. The discussion quickly turned into a fight. She was upset that he hadn't put any thought into the next step in their relationship, and this left him feeling defensive and attacked.

Five Things to Consider before You or Your Partner Make the Move

Sometimes loneliness and heartache can prompt us to want to be in the same place as our partner even though we haven't thought through the consequences of a move. Here are some things you may wish to consider when deciding if the time is right for you:

1. **Length of the relationship.** If you've only been dating a few short months, we suggest you give things more time to develop before making a huge, life-changing leap. If your partner is the right one for you, he or she will still be there if and when you're ready to make that choice.

2. **Your age.** If you're still in school, now may not be the most practical or reasonable time to move to another city. Your teens and early twenties are a good time to focus on yourself and your development as an independent person. Again, if this relationship is meant to be, it will still be there when you're ready to take it to another level.

3. **Your financial situation.** Does it make financial sense for you or your partner to move right now? Will both of you be able to find satisfying jobs with good salaries in the same city?

4. **Your career.** Is your career easily transferable to another place, or will moving disrupt the advancements you've worked so hard to achieve? What about your partner's career?

5. **Friends and family.** Certainly, the other people in your life cannot be the only factor in determining whether or not it's the right time to move, but depending on how involved these people are in your daily life, leaving them behind may bring on more heartache than dating long-distance.

Although it wasn't something Charlie had been actively considering on his own, he was ultimately open to the idea. "When I did finally take the time to really consider our future together," he says, "I got excited about what was to come." Jenn's biggest regret about how she introduced the topic was that she wasn't more patient with Charlie in terms of expectations. She expected him immediately to see that he should be the one to move, and that he needed to start looking for a job in order to make that happen. She was furious when he told her he didn't want to move.

He agrees the problem may have been in Jenn's approach. She first opened up about her thoughts during one of their late-night phone calls. They warn other couples not to make the mistake they did in having such a serious discussion over the phone. "Something as big as moving the relationship to the same locale should be talked about in person," Charlie says, "since being with that person is the ultimate goal anyway."

Stubborn thinking was another barrier to their conflict resolution. As Charlie explains, "Our first attempts at this talk didn't go very far, because we got caught in the 'I don't want to move' loop." It's no wonder. Trying to imagine uprooting your entire life is hard, especially when both partners are strong willed.

Charlie says the turning point in their decision making came when they both started talking about their long-term life goals. In order to figure out a mutually acceptable plan for the near future, they talked about their individual goals for the distant future—marriage, kids, career—and worked backward from there. Talking about long-term goals reinforced their love for each other and made working through the ugly details of the short-term transition a lot easier to bear. Once they acknowledged that they would each need to make sacrifices, working through the details became a lot easier.

Charlie and Jenn constructed their short-term plan around their life goals. First, they identified the key factors involved in making that plan, including family considerations, career aspirations, and ties to friends and community. Family ties were important to both of them, but while Charlie's family was scattered in different areas across the country, Jenn's lived in close proximity to her, and that was something she didn't want to lose. They also considered their careers. Jenn's sales career had been very successful; starting over in a new city would have required building new relationships, and it would have been difficult to reach the same level of success she had achieved in her current position. Charlie's career, on the other hand, could easily be transferred to a new area. Finally, they considered their friendships. Since Charlie had been in Jenn's hometown for a few years before moving away, he actually had quite a few friends there already. So, with all these considerations in mind, the couple decided together that it did, in fact, make the most sense for Charlie to move.

Their next step in planning was to estimate how long it might take him to find a job he would enjoy. They anticipated it would take about six months for him to find a job and make the move, and that estimate was almost exactly how it worked out. Even though Charlie had been hesitant to move at first, in the end he was glad; his new job was actually much better than the one he'd left behind, and being with Jenn was the best reward of all.

LIVING IN CLOSE QUARTERS

Once they decided that Charlie would be the one to move, the couple made another decision popular among long-distance couples who make the transition to same-city dating: moving in together. At the time, it seemed easier and more convenient for him to move into

Jenn's apartment. The couple could save money and, because they were so eager to be together, this seemed like an ideal situation. Today, they admit that choice was probably a bigger mistake than they ever could have realized at the time.

"The problem wasn't just that we were living together under one roof," Jenn says. "The problem was that we were living together under the roof that I had lived under with my two cats for almost seven years." Her apartment was small, and it was already full of the belongings she'd accumulated over her years of living there. As a result, there wasn't much room for Charlie's things, let alone Charlie.

"I wouldn't recommend going from living five hundred miles apart to sharing a two-bedroom apartment," Charlie laughs. The transition was difficult and led to a lot of arguments. "She had been living there for so long, there was little I could do except take a bit of space she had cleaned out in a closet and then find a storage unit to stash the rest of my stuff."

Tip: If you and your partner will be living in the same house or apartment after the move, declutter *before* combining your things. Who really needs two toaster ovens, two answering machines, or two ironing boards? Decide which items to keep and give the rest to charity before the big day. The move will go more smoothly, and you'll save yourselves a lot of headaches.

Space isn't the only difficulty in moving in together after living so far apart. When couples go from dating each other in distant cities to living in the same house or apartment, the transition is even more difficult than if they were dating locally but lived in separate residences. First of all, they have to get used to seeing each other every day or nearly every day, which can be wonderful, but can also be a real challenge for people who are used to their independence. In addition to making that huge leap, couples who decide to live together must also get used to a sense of sacrificing their own personal space. Sometimes that can be just too close for comfort.

We're not telling you that you and your partner shouldn't avoid living together if you feel it's the right decision for you. We are, however, suggesting you give it serious consideration before settling on that choice. Often, couples opt to live together for the sake of convenience or in an effort to save money rather than because of a sincere commitment to the relationship, and that can lead to heartache down the road. If you do go this route, anticipate some additional challenges adjusting to life after the move. It's better to be prepared for problems that may arise than to be taken by surprise when your "happily ever after" turns out to have an unexpected ending.

ALMOST PARADISE . . . BUT NOT QUITE

No relationship is perfect. If a couple expects things to be perfect when they make the shift to the same city, transitioning to a local relationship can bring some unwelcome surprises. Such was the case for Brendon and Angela. When, after a year and a half of dating long-distance, they decided that the time was right for Brendon to move to Angela's town, they were in complete bliss . . . for about two weeks. After that, the reality of daily life set in. The transition proved to be the most difficult challenge the couple had yet faced. Brendon felt he had made the more significant sacrifices for the relationship, moving to a city where he had no friends and no job. He soon discovered feelings of resentment toward the relationship and Angela, feelings he hadn't anticipated.

He had figured that settling into his new life would be somewhat challenging, but he hadn't expected that life with Angela would be anything less than what he'd imagined. Her career as a veterinarian required her to work long hours, and her schedule was often erratic. Not only was Brendon living where he had no friends and no job, but he also had an overwhelming sense that he had moved to be with a girlfriend who was never home.

He says that when he got frustrated, he focused on the good things that made him want to be with Angela in the first place. Eventually he found a job he enjoyed, and that helped ease the tension. Nevertheless, the adjustment took a great deal more time than he had ever imagined.

Tip: Before either you or your partner moves, take the time to write about your feelings. Be sure to list all your motives for making this choice. When you hit those bumpy spots on the road of love, you can look back at what you wrote and remember all the reasons you wanted to be together in the first place.

No relationship is without its share of difficulties. After all the hardships of long-distance dating, many couples mistakenly expect living in the same city will be nothing short of pure bliss. In reality, you and your partner should expect to face setbacks, regardless of where you live. Your long-distance difficulties may soon seem like a distant memory, but you'll find your relationship still requires effort to thrive and grow. The good news is that dating long-distance will have given you lots of practice in communication, patience, and love—all of which are vital to long-term happiness and relationship success.

Many of Brendon and Angela's challenges came from the fact that they had never lived in the same place, so their expectations for their local relationship were probably a bit unrealistic. But even couples who dated in the same city before dating long-distance can have difficulties when they bring their relationship back to local status. That's because, as we've said, no relationship is perfect. Problems can plague even a happy couple, whether their relationship is long-distance or local.

For Keith and Kristy, the eventual decision for Keith to move back home came with its own uncertainty and stress. When they began dating, they lived only ten minutes apart. Then Keith accepted a job in a distant city and their long-distance romance began. After two years of dating long-distance, the couple knew they were ready for a same-city commitment. They were optimistic about Keith's move and their plans for marriage. Their strong commitment eliminated any awkwardness about where they were going and what was expected.

While both were excited about the opportunity to take their relationship to a new level, they were also aware that they'd had their share of trouble before Keith accepted the out-of-town job. Getting back together presented a special challenge, since, as the couple admits, they weren't all that happy at the time he left. The idea of reuniting in the place where they had experienced troubles early on in their relationship was, at times, an intimidating prospect. Would their relationship continue to be as strong as it had become while they were dating long-distance, or would they fall back into their old patterns of relating, the patterns that had threatened their relationship before Keith moved away?

Once they were living in the same place, those concerns soon slipped away. The growth they'd experienced through long-distance dating had a profound impact on the respect and appreciation they felt for one another. At the time of this writing, Keith and Kristy have been married for eight years and credit the success of their marriage, to some degree, to the time they spent apart while they were dating.

For each couple who, like Keith and Kristy, worry that the transition to same-city dating may weaken their relationship, there are many more who mistakenly assume that having a local relationship will automatically fix the problems they experienced while dating long-distance. If you have communication problems, issues with infidelity, or incompatible goals, these problems cannot be worked out simply by living in the same place. Your relationship is what it is. If communication is a problem now, it won't improve just by changing locations. If you feel you can't trust your partner when he or she is miles away, you won't be able to trust any better just because the relationship is local. The truth is, difficulties that exist in a long-distance relationship are often exacerbated when a couple first comes to live in one place. High expectations are all too often dashed when the couple realizes they have just as many issues they need to work through—if not more. If you're not confident your relationship is in a healthy, stable place emotionally, then now is not the time to make the major life commitment of moving unless there are other compelling reasons to do so, such as career or family. Otherwise, you just may end up disappointed in your decision.

THE LIGHT AT THE END OF THE LONG-DISTANCE TUNNEL

Successfully bringing a long-distance relationship to the local level generally requires a strong commitment to seeing that relationship work out. That kind of commitment can invigorate couples with a renewed sense of love and determination. With a strong commitment in place, even the most difficult challenges of adapting to same-city life can seem easy. And, in light of the Herculean challenges most long-distance couples grow accustomed to facing on a daily basis, same-city challenges are usually relatively easy to overcome.

When Ben proposed to Sonya, he was living and working in New Mexico and she had just finished up a postgraduate program in Indiana. Once they were engaged, the challenges in their relationship lightened up. Sonya began the search for a job in New Mexico. The couple had a future together to focus on, which made everything infinitely easier. Nevertheless, planning was still difficult, and trying to merge their lifestyles was certainly not easy. They argued over where exactly they would live—he preferred the suburbs and she wanted a place in town. But in spite of their disagreements, the challenges never seemed unmanageable.

Their decision for Sonya to move had been, in large part, financial. Nevertheless, her long job search eventually became an issue. Finding a good job proved to be more difficult than she had imagined, and she didn't actually move until after their wedding. When they returned from their honeymoon, Ben went back to work in New Mexico and Sonya returned to her apartment to pack everything up. She moved into Ben's one-bedroom apartment because, until she was able to find a job there, they couldn't afford to take on higher rent.

Six Challenges of Same-City Dating

Believe it or not, intercity dating actually has some advantages, which you and your partner probably already enjoy. Before you make the leap of faith toward a same-city relationship, here are some potential pitfalls you may not be anticipating:

1. You no longer get to see your partner on his or her best behavior. This isn't really a bad thing, but it may take you by surprise the first time you see a different side to your Mr. or Ms. Right.

2. You no longer have an excuse not to visit your partner's oddball relatives.

3. Alone time is suddenly a lot harder to come by.

4. Those cute little quirks can seem downright annoying when you're with someone every day.

5. All of your stuff + all of your partner's stuff = a lot of stuff you don't need or have space for.

6. It's harder to miss someone you see every day.

Sharing such a small space did present some difficulties at the outset. "We were used to being very independent and had our own way of doing things," Sonya says. "Our biggest fight during our first year of marriage was a recurring disagreement over the best way to load the dishwasher."

For Sonya and Ben, the experience of long-distance dating strengthened their commitment to one another. But both say they wouldn't recommend dating long-distance to anyone unless the relationship has real promise for moving forward. "If this is something with real potential, then a long-distance relationship is worth exploring. But you can't do it forever," Sonya advises. "There should be a natural point where you need to ask whether or not you have serious potential for a future together. If that answer is no, you should end the relationship."

What if the answer is yes? Hopefully, this book has provided you with some strategies you can use to help make your long-distance relationship a fun, rewarding experience for you and your partner. As Sonya puts it, "You can have a long-distance relationship and still have a wonderful life. I loved dating long-distance for the time it lasted, but I wouldn't have wanted to do it forever."

Now that she and Ben are together, Sonya says the rewards have been well worth the wait. The couple has been married over a year. They appreciate being together every day without the stress of knowing one of them will be leaving at the end of the weekend, and that small truth feels like a real blessing.

In fact, ultimately bringing the relationship together in the same place is one of the most joyful experiences a long-distance couple can share. The chance to live a life together is the ultimate reward for the sacrifices and challenges of a long-distance relationship, and it is this chance that gives us hope and keeps us going when problems seem insurmountable.

Long-distance dating can be a lot of things: it can be challenging, to be certain—even lonely, alienating, and depressing at times. But just when you're ready to throw in the towel, you may also discover that your long-distance relationship has its share of rewards, too: independence, mutual appreciation, improved communication, and a deepening commitment. Those virtues are often enough to carry a relationship through to long-term success. In fact, our marriage is the strong, loving union it is today in large part thanks to the communication and goal-setting skills we developed as a long-distance couple.

Whatever your situation, we wish you the best of luck. Intercity dating can be one of the most challenging endeavors a couple will face, but take heart: no matter what the outcome of your long-distance relationship, you are almost certain to learn about your partner and yourself in ways you never imagined. With any luck, you'll learn you've found an open, loving soul mate who is willing to go the distance for you and your relationship. What's more, you just may discover those same qualities in yourself.

INDEX

ABOUT THE AUTHORS

Chris Bell and **Kate Brauer-Bell** fell in love in Cincinnati, a few weeks after Chris had accepted a job five hundred miles away, thus beginning nineteen months of phone calls, emails, and countless trips by car or plane. Married since 2003, they now live together in Maineville, Ohio, with their son, George, and a second child on the way.